FRANCE

Ethel Caro Gofen/Blandine Pengili Reymann

BENCHMARK BOOKS

MARSHALL CAVENDISH
NEW YORK

PICTURE CREDITS
Cover photo: © Trip/Ask Images
AFP: 51, 52, 55, 60, 108, 127 • ANA Press Agency: 11, 38, 39, 84 • Art Directors & Trip: 1,
13, 30, 34, 48, 74, 90, 110 • Jan Butchofsky/Houserstock: 64, 76, 79, 120 • Getty Images/
Hulton Archive: 21, 29 • Haga Library: 56, 112 • HBL Network: 3, 9, 18, 26, 103, 104 • Dave
G. Houser/Houserstock: 6, 8, 59, 125 • Hutchison Library: 75 • Andre Laubier: 115 • Les
Voyageurs: 22, 63, 65, 71, 72, 85, 96, 126 • Life File Photographic Library: 4, 7, 12, 14, 15,
16, 24, 27, 31, 33, 44, 66, 68, 86, 98, 100, 102, 105, 107, 109, 111, 114, 116, 121, 122, 123, 128,
129 • Lonely Planet Images: 50, 92, 130, 131 • MacQuitty International Collection: 36, 77
• Marco Polo: 5, 10, 17, 40, 41, 42, 43, 45, 47, 57, 58, 61, 69, 78, 80, 82, 93, 94, 95, 97, 106,
117, 118

ACKNOWLEDGMENTS
With thanks to Daniela Bleichmar for her expert reading of this manuscript

PRECEDING PAGE
French children in traditional dress at the Obernai Festival in Strasbourg

Marshall Cavendish Corporation
99 White Plains Road
Tarrytown, NY 10591
Website: www.marshallcavendish.com

Originated and designed by
Times Books International, an imprint of
Times Media Private Limited, a member of
Times International Publishing

Printed in Singapore

Library of Congress Cataloging-in-Publication Data
Gofen, Ethel, 1937–
    France / by Ethel Caro Gofen and Blandine Pengili Reymann. 2nd ed.
        p. cm.—(Cultures of the world—2nd edition)
    Summary: Introduces the geography, history, economy, cultures, and people of
France. Includes bibliographical references and index.
    ISBN 0-7614-1498-3
    1. France—Juvenile literature. [1. France.] I. Reymann, Blandine Pengili. II. Title.
III. Series: Cultures of the world 2nd ed.)
DC33.G54 2002
944—dc21   2002011624

7 6 5 4 3

CONTENTS

A reclining Neptune, one of many sculptures decorating the parks and ponds of the Palace of Versailles.

Saint-Tropez on the Côte d'Azur is a favorite vacation spot for thousands of French people and tourists.

INTRODUCTION

FRANCE IS A LAND of incredible beauty. From the streets of Paris to the Alpine glaciers, from the beaches of Normandy to the flower-strewn hills of Provence, the French landscape is varied and picturesque.

Energetic, cultured, and well-educated, the French have mastered the art of living joyfully. Their achievements in science, architecture, literature, painting, fashion, cooking, and wine-making have dazzled the rest of the world. Having experienced many different forms of government in their tumultuous history, the French have learned to defend the rights of the individual against all forms of tyranny and have upheld the ideals of Liberty, Equality, and Brotherhood.

This book, part of the series *Cultures of the World*, provides insights into the lifestyle of the French people and their dynamic intellectual and cultural achievements.

GEOGRAPHY

FRANCE IS BLESSED WITH FERTILE SOIL and a pleasant climate. A great diversity of landforms exists: snowcapped mountains, wide plains, dense forests, windblown seacoasts, extinct volcanic cones, ancient underground caves, and sunny Mediterranean beaches.

The country is roughly hexagonal in shape and covers 212,005 square miles (549,090 square km). It is about 600 miles (966 km) long and 600 miles at its widest point. Corsica, southeast of the mainland in the Mediterranean Sea, accounts for 3,352 square miles (8,682 square km) of the total land area.

France's bordering neighbors are Belgium, Luxembourg, and Germany to the northeast, Switzerland and Italy to the east and southeast, Andorra to the south, and Spain to the southwest.

Most of France's boundaries are natural: the Atlantic Ocean and the Bay of Biscay to the west, the English Channel to the northwest (separating France from England), and the Mediterranean Sea to the southeast. On the mainland, the Pyrenees Mountains lead into Spain, the Alps and the Jura Mountains border Switzerland, and more Alpine peaks act as a barrier between France and Italy. The Rhine River flows between France and Germany. Where no natural barriers exist, France has in the past been vulnerable to invasion by foreign armies.

Above: **The coast of Brittany contains many tranquil little coves that get crowded only during summer vacations.**

Opposite: **Collioure is a Catalan village on the Languedoc-Roussillon coast.**

This restored windmill in Burgundy still produces flour. Burgundy, near the center of France, is a region known for its wine, Roman ruins, beautiful chateaux, and quaint medieval towns.

MAIN GEOGRAPHICAL REGIONS

The widely varied landscapes of mainland France can be divided into different geographical regions, each with its own unique beauty.

THE BRITTANY-NORMANDY HILLS lie in northwestern France across the eroded remains of ancient rock. Low hills and rolling plains are covered with relatively infertile soil. The rugged coastline is dotted with many bays and is home to both tiny fishing villages and the major seaports of Le Havre and Cherbourg.

Important products of this region include apples, used to make cider and an alcoholic drink called Calvados, dairy foods such as Camembert cheese and Normandy butter, and fish.

Brittany, with the highest percentage of Roman Catholic churchgoers of any French region, also has a small group of extremist Bretons who want to separate from the rest of the country. The ancient Celtic language is still spoken here, and mysterious standing stones recall the ancestors.

THE FRENCH ALPS are part of a great chain that extends across Europe. In France, the Alpine peaks, known as the Massif du Mont Blanc, are crowned by the highest peak in the chain—Mont Blanc. Also in eastern France, the folded limestone Jura Mountains extend into Switzerland. The water power from these mountain streams is harnessed to generate hydroelectric power. The French Alps also boast many ski resorts. The highest point in France is Mont Blanc at 15,771 feet (4,807 m) in the French Alps. The lowest area in France is the Rhône River delta at 7 feet (2 m).

THE RHÔNE-SAÔNE VALLEY in the Rhône-Alpes region is a major wine-producing area. In the southeast of France, it is an extensive valley separating the Alps from the central plateau of France. The river in the north is called the Saône, becoming the Rhône in the south. Tourists flock to the Rhône valley to ski in the Alps, visit the historic cities of Provence, and ride horses in the Camargue. This area is dominated by the industrial city of Lyon, second only to Paris in size. Lyon has been famous, for many centuries, for its cooking and its silk and synthetic fabrics.

THE NORTHERN FRANCE PLAINS include the capital city of Paris, the economic, cultural, intellectual, and industrial center of France.

Surrounding Paris is the Paris Basin, which includes the historical regions of Beauce, Brie, Île-de-France (one of France's most populous areas), Soissonnais, and Valois. Drained by the Seine, the Paris Basin

Snow-covered ski cabins in Savoy, in the Rhône-Alpes region. This is excellent skiing, snowboarding, mountain climbing, and mountain biking country.

Nice is a prosperous town, and its port is always teeming with yachts and other pleasure boats.

consists of lowlands made up of sedimentary beds of limestone, sand, and clay. The soil here is loamy and fertile, bearing rich farmland and dense forests that support a dense population. The Paris Basin, together with southwestern France, is where most of France's grain is produced.

THE FRENCH RIVIERA is an international playground of great beauty. A visitor to this region can experience many altitudes, from mountains and charming hill towns down to a coastal plains and sandy beaches. Marseille, France's chief seaport, and the tiny independent country of Monaco are in this area, as are the renowned resort cities of Nice and Cannes. Awesome Roman ruins, medieval buildings, ancient olive groves, and even bullfight arenas mark the inland region of Provence-Alpes-Côte d'Azur. Many famous French artists have tried to capture the luminous daylight of the French Rivieria.

THE NORTHEASTERN PLATEAUS include the populous and industrialized provinces of Alsace and Lorraine. These plateaus are crossed by the Ardennes and Vosges mountain ranges. Farms and vineyards dominate the lower slopes and valleys. Lorraine has iron and coal deposits and Alsace textile and chemical industries. This is also a major milk and beef-producing area.

THE MASSIF CENTRAL is the largest of France's geographical regions, covering one-sixth of the country. High granite plateaus are cut in many places by deep gorges. Extinct volcanic cones known as *puys* ("PWEE"),

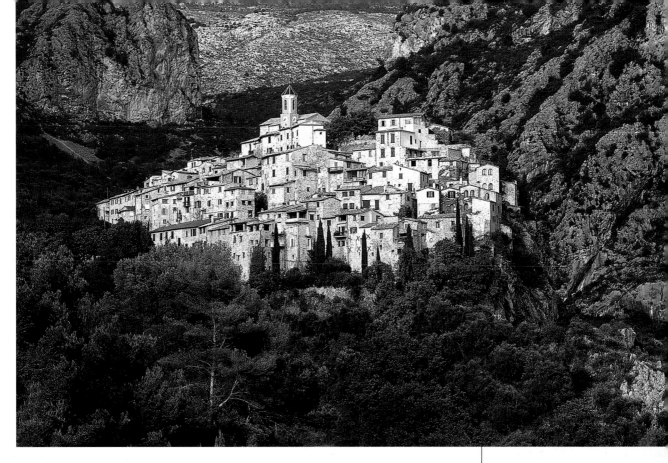

some topped with chapels or religious statues, are a striking feature of the area. At Vichy, naturally hot mineral springs have led to the development of health spas. Vichy's mineral water is also bottled for export to distant countries. The soil is poor in most of the Massif Central, and the area is thinly populated. In recent years, many people from this part of France have moved to Paris to look for work.

THE PYRENEES MOUNTAINS separate France and Spain in a sparsely populated region of the southwest. Many of the sheer mountain peaks top 10,000 feet (3,048 m). Farmers raise cattle and sheep in this area. The Midi-Pyrénées town of Lourdes, with its reputation for miraculous cures, attracts millions of Roman Catholic pilgrims annually.

THE AQUITAINE BASIN is a lowland region known for its fruit orchards, the Bordeaux wine industry, oil and natural gas fields, steel mills, and chemical factories. Extensive forests, rolling plains, huge sand dunes, and beaches are characteristic features of this area.

Peillon is a picturesque, perched village, about 12 miles (20 km) north of Nice. This fortified medieval village sits on top of a narrow rocky peak. It is considered one of the most beautiful perched villages of the Côte d'Azur.

A COUNTRY NOURISHED BY WATER

Throughout French history, rivers have brought fertility to the land and nourished flourishing centers of population. These rivers, with their lesser tributaries and a vast system of linking canals, have enabled the French to cross their country by boat and barge.

France's most important rivers include the Loire, the Seine, the Garonne, the Rhône, the Saône, the Rhine, the Somme, and the Marne. The Loire is the longest river entirely within France—632 miles (1,017 km) long. Glorious chateaus, or castles, adorn its banks. The slow-moving Seine connects Paris with the Atlantic Ocean. The wine-producing seaport of Bordeaux lies on the Garonne, its location making it an ideal home for merchants and shipbuilders.

Lyon lies at the point where the Rhône and Saône rivers meet, and its heart is a peninsula between the two rivers. Since the Rhône-Saône Valley receives relatively little rainfall, the Rhône, originating from Lake Geneva in Switzerland, provides both hydroelectric power and irrigation to farms and vineyards in the region. Hydroelectric power for Alsace and Lorraine is supplied by the Rhine, which flows along the French-German border.

A complex system of canals aids the movement of goods between smaller cities and towns. Picturesque examples are the Nantes-Brest Canal in Brittany and Pays de la Loire, the Canal du Nivernais in Burgundy, and the Canal du Midi, running from Toulouse in the Midi-Pyrénées region to the Languedoc-Roussillon coast.

TERRITORIES

France is divided into 22 administrative regions: Alsace, Aquitaine, Auvergne, Brittany, Burgundy, Centre, Champagne-Ardenne, Corse, Franche-Comté, Île-de-France, Languedoc-Roussillon, Limousin, Lorraine, Lower Normandy, Midi-Pyrénées, Nord-Pas-de-Calais, Pays de la Loire, Picardy, Poitou-Charentes, Provence-Alpes-Côte d'Azur, Rhône-Alpes, and Upper Normandy. These regions are subdivided into 96 *départements* ("day-par-tun-MAHN"), or departments.

From its colonial past, France has jurisdiction over many overseas departments and territories: French Guiana in South America, Guadeloupe and Martinique in the Caribbean, Réunion and Mayotte in the Indian Ocean, and Saint-Pierre and Miquelon in the North Atlantic Ocean. Areas also dependent on France include French Polynesia and New Caledonia.

Bora Bora, French Polynesia, in the southern Pacific Ocean.

CORSICA SEEKS A SEPARATE IDENTITY

The island of Corsica lies in the Mediterranean Sea about 105 miles (170 km) from the southern French coast and 56 miles (90 km) from Italy. Over the centuries, Corsica has been conquered by invaders from Greece, Rome, Pisa, and Genoa. In 1768 Genoa sold its rights to Corsica to the French, and the island became a *département* of the French Republic.

Corsica's coast is marked by steep, rocky cliffs leading to rugged mountains. Poor soil and heavy forests limit the amount of land given to agricultural use. Some inhabitants fish and raise sheep, and others cultivate crops or work in industries based on hydroelectric development. Tobacco-growing supports about one-quarter of the economy. Tourism is the primary source of the island's income. Its sandy beaches, palm trees, and dramatic scenery draw visitors from around the world. Many villages have remained virtually unchanged for hundreds of years. Corsica is covered by lush vegetation, notably the macchia underbrush. The island's plants produce a fragrance that even carries out to sea, giving the island the name "The Scented Isle."

Napoleon Bonaparte, who became emperor of France, was born in the capital city of Ajaccio on August 15, 1769.

In Corsica, traditional loyalties to family and clan have led to lengthy, sometimes deadly, vendettas. In fact, the word "vendetta," meaning a hereditary blood feud, came into the English language from Corsica.

More recently, Corsican zeal has inspired a guerrilla battle for greater autonomy from France and for cultural recognition. The Corsican language, a form of Italian, is widely spoken at home, although France has banned it from the schools. Corsican nationalists, particularly those from the Front de Libération Nationale de la Corse (National Liberation Front of Corsica), have not hesitated to use terrorist tactics to further their separatist aims.

In 1991 Corsica was granted the status of territorial collectivity. In 1999 the controversial Matignon Process was started, involving representatives of the French government and leaders of Corsica, to grant Corsica greater legislative autonomy by 2004.

CLIMATE

France's climate is generally moderate, as a result of the effects of the North Atlantic Drift from the west and the Mediterranean Sea in the south, and favorable to cultivation. There are three main climatic zones: the oceanic northwest with constant temperatures, the Mediterranean southeast with warm winters and generally fine weather, and the continental northeast with cold winters and light rain.

The Provence region has a warm climate that supports lush tropical greenery.

Western France receives winds from over the Atlantic Ocean that bring rain, cool winters, and moderate summers. The Gulf Stream in the Atlantic Ocean tempers the climate and makes it more moderate than at comparable latitudes in North America. Light misty rain is common throughout most of the year.

Inland, there is a more pronounced seasonal difference, with hotter summers, colder winters, and clearly defined wet and dry periods.

Eastern France and the mountainous areas experience severe winters and stormy summers. The Vosges Mountains contribute to Alsace's sharp, cold winters and warm to hot summers. Alpine peaks above 9,000 feet (2,743 m) and Pyrenean peaks above 10,000 feet (3,048 m) are snow-capped all year round.

The French Riviera has a dry, warm climate. Occasionally, cold northerly winds known as mistral blow through southeastern France at a brutal 65 miles (105 km) per hour—enough force to damage crops.

There is a profusion of flowers in France. Some are used in the perfume industry; others, like the sunflower, are used to produce oil.

FLORA AND FAUNA

More than a quarter of France is covered with trees and plants. These vary with the climate from one part of the country to another. In the northern and central regions, forests of oak, chestnut, pine, and beech trees are common. In the low-lying marshes, willows, poplar, and cypress trees may be found.

On the western border, carefully planted pine forests thrive where swamps have been drained. Brittany's landscape, so commonly a bleak expanse of moors with scrubby brush and stunted trees, contrasts greatly with the Provençal landscape of ancient olive trees and verdant grapevines and fruit trees. In other parts of France, cypress, Spanish chestnut, and ash trees form thick groves and forests. Evergreens such as cushion pine, dwarf pine, and juniper flourish in parts of the Alps.

Wheat, barley, and corn are among the chief crops in France. Lavender, thyme, and other herbs, buried truffles, and mushrooms in rich variety scent the fields and flavor the tables of France.

The Atlantic and Mediterranean coasts offer a colorful palette of shellfish and other sea creatures. Oysters and lobsters caught off the coasts of Normandy and Brittany, and trout and salmon caught off the southern coasts delight diners throughout the country.

Flamingos, herons, and storks ripple the lake waters of nature reserves in the province of Lorraine. Wild animals include the brown bear, wild boar, polecat, wildcat, and deer. Majestic white horses and black bulls roam the nature reserves of the marshy Camargue region. Smaller mammals commonly seen in the French countryside include badgers, bats, beavers, foxes, hares, hedgehogs, moles, rabbits, squirrels, and weasels. Farmers depend on cattle, chickens, hogs, and sheep for a living. The rare chamois and marmot can be spotted in the Alps and the lynx in the Pyrenees Mountains.

The white horses bred in the Camargue region are smaller than other breeds. Their endurance, agility, and rapid reflexes make them ideal for working with bulls.

HISTORY

TWO THEMES dominate French history. One is the drive to forge a unified nation out of diverse peoples; the other is the quest for glory. France wanted, and still wants, to embody the most cultured and enlightened civilization in the world.

EARLY SETTLERS

Prehistoric cave dwellers are estimated to have inhabited France as far back as 750,000 years ago. The first tribes known to have invaded the region some 2,000 to 4,000 years ago were the Celts. Today, megalithic monuments and Celtic words in the French language recall them.

The Romans named Celtic territories Gaul. These territories included modern-day France, northern Italy, the southern Netherlands, and Belgium. The Roman emperor Julius Caesar defeated the Gallic chief Vercingetorix in 52 B.C., and the Romans ruled Gaul for about 500 years. They left behind road systems, towns, cities, a legal system, taxes, and winemaking.

In the fifth century A.D., the Germanic Visigoths, Burgundians, and Franks pushed into the area that is now France. The Visigoths settled in the Provence and Aquitaine regions; the Burgundians occupied much of the Rhône Valley; and the Franks settled in the northeast. The Frankish king Clovis I of the Merovingian dynasty defeated the last Roman ruler in 486 and later established the capital of his kingdom in Paris. By the seventh century, the Merovingian dynasty was replaced by the Frankish Carolingian dynasty. The greatest Carolingian ruler was Charlemagne, who ruled from 771 to 814. Conquering territories in Spain, Germany, and northern Italy, he was crowned Holy Roman Emperor in 800. After his death, his empire was divided among his three grandsons into Germany; Belgium, the Netherlands, France's Alsace and Lorraine regions, and northern Italy; and France (mainly Aquitaine and the region around Paris).

Opposite: **The Bridge of the Gard is a giant bridge-aqueduct. It was built by the Romans in about 19 B.C. to carry water to the city of Nîmes over the Gard River in southern France. Three tiers of arches rise to a height of 155 feet (47 m). The first tier is composed of six arches, the largest spanning the river; the second tier is composed of 11 arches of the same dimensions; the third, carrying the conduit, is composed of 35 smaller arches.**

THE MIDDLE AGES

After the Carolingian dynasty, the Capetians ruled France from 987 to 1328 with perseverance and a practical sense for politics. They were descendents of Robert the Strong, count of Anjou and Blois. Robert's great-grandson, Hugh Capet, the first Capetian king, was succeeded by 13 kings. They laid the foundation for the French nation-state but feudalism weakened their power.

Noble lords received royal land in exchange for service to the king, and many became more powerful than the king. By the 11th century, France was a mosaic of feudal domains. The most powerful was that of William II (later called William the Conqueror), Duke of Normandy, who invaded England in 1066 and became King of England.

During the Crusades from the 11th to the 13th centuries, the Capetian kings regained power over their ambitious vassals. When Christians left France for the Holy Land to fight against the Muslims, the monarchy took the opportunity to seize the land and power of the crusading nobles. By the 1330s, France was the most powerful kingdom in Western Europe. During Capetian reign, intellectual life made great progress. Universities were founded, and the University of Paris became the center of philosophical and theological studies in the Christian world.

A political struggle for power, in particular over the legitimate succession to the French crown, led France and England to war in 1337. Periodic battles continued for 116 years, known collectively as the Hundred Years' War. Some say that this war marked the end of English attempts to control continental territory. The war was interrupted by a monstrous plague, the Black Death, which killed one-third of all the people in Europe. When fighting resumed, the English nearly conquered all of France. However, the religious zeal, patriotism, purity, and courage of the young Joan of Arc helped turn the tide of the war.

SAINT JOAN OF ARC

Saint Joan of Arc, also called the Maid of Orléans, was born in 1412 to a farming family in the northern village of Domrémy in Lorraine. At 13, Joan claimed to have heard voices from God directing her to be a good girl. When she was 17, the voices told her to leave home and save France and the king.

Joan was determined to obey these voices. She sought an audience with the dauphin, the eldest son of the late King Charles VI. The dauphin had been disinherited by the English in the Treaty of Troyes in 1420. Joan convinced the uncrowned king and his advisors that the siege of Orléans would be the battle to end the Hundred Years' War. Dressed in armor, Joan led French troops to victory at Orléans on May 8, 1429. She then led French troops and the dauphin through English-occupied territory to Reims for his coronation as King Charles VII.

During the siege of Paris in 1430, Joan was captured by the Duke of Burgundy and delivered to the English. Holding fast to her faith and denying that the voices she had heard were demonic, she was tried by an English-dominated Church court and condemned as a witch. Joan was burned at the stake in Rouen on May 30, 1431. She was just 19 years old.

It is said that the spirit of the Maid of Orléans enabled the French army, who then believed that God was on their side, to finally drive the English out of France, except for the port of Calais in the far north. Joan had also revived France's devotion to the monarchy. Almost 500 years after her death, in 1920, Joan of Arc was canonized by the Roman Catholic Church as St. Joan of Arc.

THE SUN KING

Louis XIV was the personification of the quest for glory and the embodiment of absolute power. King of France from 1643 to 1715, he viewed himself as God's representative on Earth. Louis extended France's eastern borders and brought the nobility, the justice system, and the military all under his control. Much of his success, however, could be attributed to his brillant counselor—Jean-Baptiste Colbert.

Louis built a magnificent palace at Versailles, still one of the glories of Europe. He attracted the most gifted artists, architects, writers, engineers, and scientists to his court. However, his disregard for the common French people, his decadence, and his persecution of the French Protestants, causing many of them to flee France, set the scene for the eventual downfall of the monarchy.

THE REFORMATION

Roughly, the boundaries of present-day France were established by 1500 under the Valois kings. It was also during their reign that the ideals of the Renaissance spread to France from Italy.

A religious movement called the Reformation in the second half of the 16th century gave rise to Protestantism. The reformer Martin Luther's works first appeared in France in 1519, and anti-Catholic placards began to appear in Paris and other French towns by the 1530s. This led to civil war and Catholic persecution of the French Protestants, called Huguenots. Thousands of Huguenots were massacred, 3,000 at once in Paris on St. Bartholomew's Day in 1572.

The wars ended when Huguenot leader Henri of Navarre converted to Roman Catholicism and was crowned King Henri IV in 1594, the first of the Bourbon kings. Henri signed the Edict of Nantes in 1598, granting the Huguenots religious and civil liberties.

The next two kings, Louis XIII and Louis XIV, were absolute monarchs, holding great power.

THE FRENCH REVOLUTION

The seeds of the French Revolution were planted in part by philosophers of the Enlightenment spreading new ideals of government and justice and in part by the anger of the rapidly growing but generally impoverished population with the injustices that existed in society.

In 1789 King Louis XVI tried to deal with the crisis by assembling the old Estates General, consisting of three classes: clergy, nobles, and commoners. But the clergy and nobles clashed with the newer class of commoners, who broke away and declared themselves the legal National Assembly. The king mustered 20,000 royal troops to Paris. Believing that he was planning to suppress the new assembly, an angry mob stormed the Bastille prison on July 14. Peasants revolted in the countryside and fighting erupted in the cities. The National Assembly seized control. Traditional privileges were removed from the nobles and clergy, and the feudal system ended. In 1791 a new constitution changed the absolute monarchy into a constitutional monarchy. The National Assembly divided the country into 83 *départements* of roughly similar size.

King Louis and Queen Marie-Antoinette tried to flee the country but were arrested and forced to sign the new constitution. Royalists and counterrevolutionaries opposed the assembly, and in April 1792 France went to war against Austria and Prussia. Fear of counterrevolutionaries in the Parisian prisons led to the mass execution of more than a thousand prisoners. The king and queen were killed.

The French Revolution then entered a second, radical phase. Extremist Jacobins under Georges-Jacques Danton, Jean-Paul Marat, and Maximilien Robespierre rose to power and set up the Commune of Paris. Robespierre led the Committee of Public Safety, which inaugurated the Terror, a wave of massacres and executions of enemies of the Revolution. Tens

"Men are born and remain free and equal in rights. Social distinctions may be based only on considerations of the common good."

— The first article of the 1789 French Declaration of the Rights of Man and the Citizen. This declaration was inspired by the American Declaration of Independence of 1776.

NAPOLEON BONAPARTE

During the French Revolution a young officer named Napoleon Bonaparte, born in Corsica, rapidly rose to power. In 1799 Napoleon led a successful coup against the government. He quickly installed a new form of government, the Consulate, with himself as first consul.

Napoleon gave France an enlightened civil code (the Napoleonic Code of 1804), religious tolerance, and elite schools, or *grandes écoles* ("GRAHND-dzay-KOHL"). He created an efficient central government with a stable currency and reasonably just taxes and founded the Bank of France. He named himself emperor in 1804 and, with his wife Josephine, left a lasting impact on French style and fashion.

A great military strategist and heroic leader, Napoleon conquered most of Europe. But his troops were finally stopped in Russia in 1812 by harsh winter weather and a shortage of food. After his defeat in Russia and losing the decisive Battle of Leipzig in 1813, he abdicated in 1814 and was exiled on the island of Elba. A brief return to power, between March and June 1815, ended with Napoleon's military defeat at Waterloo by British and Prussian forces. Napoleon was banished to the island of St. Helena in the Atlantic where he died in 1821.

of thousands were guillotined in the name of "*Liberté, Égalité, Fraternité*" ("Liberty, Equality, and Brotherhood"). In 1792 the National Convention abolished the monarchy and proclaimed the First French Republic. France exported revolution abroad to form "sister republics" in Western Europe. Switzerland, northern Italy, and the Netherlands came under French influence. An anti-France alliance, consisting of Austria, Prussia, Great Britain, the Netherlands, Sardinia, and Spain, was formed. A temporary government, the Directory, controlled France from 1795 to 1799. Many elections, revolts, and purges followed. Napoleon Bonaparte emerged from this chaos to lead France against its enemies and expand its borders.

THE SEARCH FOR STABLE GOVERNMENT

After Napoleon's defeat, Austrian, Prussian, Russian, French, and British delegates reorganized Europe during the Congress of Vienna (1814–15) and restored the French borders to what they had been in 1792. In the years that followed, France underwent several political changes: it was first governed by a constitutional monarchy, then by an authoritarian empire, and finally it became a republic.

First, the monarchy was restored with two more kings of the Bourbon royal family. Their rule was replaced in 1848 by the Second Republic, with Frenchmen demanding a republic and the right to vote. The last king, Louis-Philippe, abdicated in 1848. Napoleon Bonaparte's nephew, Louis-Napoleon Bonaparte, established the Second Empire and was proclaimed Emperor Napoleon III in 1852.

During the Second Empire, industrial production doubled, foreign trade tripled, the first investment banks opened, and French engineers built bridges, railways, docks, and sewage systems at home and abroad. Napoleon also liberalized the political system. His reign ended with French defeat in the Franco-Prussian War (1870–71). The postwar treaty forced France to give much of Alsace and Lorraine to the new German empire. The people ousted Napoleon III, and a new constitution became the basis for the Third Republic.

From 1899 to 1905 a coalition of left-wing and center parties provided France with political stability and fostered economic growth. France established a powerful colonial empire in Africa and Asia, rivalled only by Britain's. *La belle époque* (the Beautiful Era) is how the years between 1890 and 1914 are remembered. The period witnessed developments in education, the flowering of Paris as a social and art capital, the rise of labor unions, and the separation of church and state.

The Suez Canal is an engineering marvel connecting the Mediterranean Sea and the Red Sea. It allows ships to sail directly between the Mediterranean Sea and the Indian Ocean, rather than having to round Africa via the Cape of Good Hope. It took the French Suez Canal Company 11 years to build and was completed in 1869 under the direction of Ferdinand de Lesseps.

p26: Triumphant rejoicing at the Place de L'Etoile, the public space extending out from the Arc de Triomphe, after the liberation of Paris in 1944.

TWO WORLD WARS

The massive loss of life in World War I, the worldwide economic depression, and defeat by Germany in World War II marked one of the lowest periods in French history.

In 1907 France entered into a diplomatic agreement, the Triple Entente, with Britain and Russia. Germany invaded France shortly after World War I began in 1914. Much of the war was fought in France; about 1.3 million French perished, and 1 million became disabled.

Soldiers suffered the horrors of trench warfare and new technologies of death: bombs dropped from airplanes, and poison gas. Economic growth was set back a decade, and production fell to 60 percent of prewar levels.

After the war, Alsace and Lorraine were restored to France, but the French economy had suffered greatly. Recovery was dependent on German reparations. To rebuild manpower, immigration restrictions were relaxed and about 2 million foreign workers entered France.

In the 1930s the world entered into an economic depression. This led to political turmoil. In France, right-wing movements grew in strength. In Germany, Nazi leader Adolf Hitler ascended to the chancellorship, supported by millions of jobless and dissatisfied Germans.

In September 1939 Germany invaded Poland, dragging France and Britain into World War II. In May 1940 Germany invaded France. Unprepared, France fell quickly, and Germany occupied the northern two-thirds of France, including Paris. Southern France remained in French hands for a while, with a German-controlled puppet government in Vichy under Marshal Pétain, a World War I hero. In 1942 southern France was also occupied.

During this time, some French collaborated with the Germans for their own advancement. Others formed an underground resistance. On June 6, 1944, Allied soldiers landed in Normandy and liberated France, with the aid of local Resistance forces.

After the war, a new constitution written by the National Assembly in 1945 created the Fourth Republic, which was led by General Charles de Gaulle. That year, Frenchwomen voted for the first time. France rebuilt its economy with much help from the U.S. Marshall Plan. In 1949 France became a charter member of the North Atlantic Treaty Organization (NATO). The Allied victory over Germany ultimately restored France's prewar boundaries.

A war memorial. Some of the heaviest fighting in both world wars took place on French soil.

POSTWAR FRANCE

France lost important colonies during World War II. Indochina was taken by the Japanese during the war; after the war, France regained control only of southern Indochina. After eight years of bloody struggle, France withdrew, and the former colony was divided into the People's Republic of Kampuchea (Cambodia), Laos, and North and South Vietnam. In 1954 rebellion broke out in Algeria, and a long and brutal struggle ensued. Fear that the rebellion would spread to Morocco and Tunisia led the French government to make drastic concessions to these two countries, which gained independence in 1956. The costly war in Algeria lasted through the 1950s, sharply dividing the French and inspiring terrorist violence. In 1962 Algeria finally gained independence.

The president who succeeded Charles de Gaulle was Georges Pompidou (1969–74). He made significant contributions to the development of France's nuclear proficiency and a new defense plan. Valéry Giscard d'Estaing, leader of the Independent Republican Party, took over with a coalition government. With the election of President François Mitterrand of the Socialist Party in 1981, government ownership of businesses increased. Mitterrand was elected for a second term in 1988. Socialists also controlled Parliament until 1986, when Jacques Chirac, the conservative mayor of Paris, became prime minister. (This was the first case of "cohabitation," with a prime minister from a different coalition than the president.) In the election of 1993, conservative Édouard Balladur became prime minister under François Mitterrand. In 1995 Jacques Chirac was elected president for seven years, and in 1997 socialist Lionel Jospin was appointed prime minister for the next five years. In 2002 Jacques Chirac was reelected to the presidency for five years by a resounding 82 percent against right-wing extremist and xenophobe Jean-Marie Le Pen.

GENERAL CHARLES DE GAULLE

One of the monumental figures in 20th-century France was General Charles de Gaulle. During World War II, in exile in England and sentenced in absentia to death by a French court, he courageously opposed the Nazis and formed the Free French Forces, sending radio broadcasts to his French compatriots from London. His heroic resistance movement spread throughout France.

De Gaulle headed two provisional governments after the war but resigned in 1946. He opposed the Fourth French Republic and its constitution, which he did not think improved on the Third Republic's inadequacies. In 1947 de Gaulle formed the Rassemblement du Peuple Français (Rally of the French People), which obtained 120 seats in the National Assembly but was later disbanded.

An opportunity for de Gaulle to return to power presented itself in 1958 when the insurrection in Algiers brought France to the brink of civil war. De Gaulle was elected to a seven-year term as president on December 21, 1958. He developed a new constitution, establishing the Fifth Republic. Under this constitution, the president's powers were greatly increased, while those of the parliament were reduced.

De Gaulle worked hard to make France a strong, independent power, free from the domination of either the United States or the Soviet Union. He saw France as the rightful leader of Europe. He recognized the People's Republic of China, encouraged an independent French nuclear-weapons program, and removed all French troops from NATO. De Gaulle urged France to join the European Common Market, while keeping Great Britain out.

De Gaulle was a tall, striking man, who seemed in his very person to symbolize French glory. The French people admired his courage and integrity. Yet many eventually began to resent his arrogance that made him seem at times more a king than a president. De Gaulle's leadership survived student uprisings and widespread strikes that paralyzed the economy. He finally resigned in 1969 after the French rejected his constitutional reforms. He quietly retired to his country home, where he died the following year.

GOVERNMENT

DEBATING THE BEST FORM OF GOVERNMENT for their country is one of the passions of the French people. They sit at café tables or in the public square and talk endlessly about politics, French leaders, and how France could be better governed.

French philosophers and leaders have aspired over the centuries toward different ideals of good government. At many points in French history, kings, courtiers, peasants, and soldiers of every class have engaged in bloody battles for the power to rule. Over the course of its history, France has witnessed many different forms of government, including feudalism, absolute monarchy, constitutional monarchy, empire, and now parliamentary democracy.

Left: **The offices of the Conseil d'Etat, the supreme body consulted by the French government before a new law is passed.**

Opposite: **The country town hall may be housed in a charming building with great historical character, such as this one in Le Touquet on the northern French coast.**

NATIONAL GOVERNMENT

"Every French presidency takes on some of the flavor of a royal court. ... The French adore the political leader who shows a mystic identification with the French soil, with the countryside, the nation's rural roots. ... The political leader has to communicate a deep sense of history, to intone the great themes of the French nation."

—Richard Bernstein

Until the French Revolution of 1789, France was a monarchy ruled by a king. Since then France has been governed according to its written constitution. The current constitution is an amended form of the 1958 constitution of the Fifth Republic.

France is a democratic republic, with its capital in Paris. The government since 1958 has been known as the Fifth Republic. The president of this parliamentary democracy was previously elected by all voters (citizens age 18 or older) for a seven-year term. (In 2002 this term of office was shortened to five years.) The president appoints the prime minister, who then recommends to the president the other ministers who form the Council of Ministers, the French cabinet. The prime minister oversees the day-to-day affairs of the government, while the president, as head of state, focuses on the direction of national policy and foreign affairs.

France's national government has three branches. The executive branch is headed by the president and the prime minister. The legislative branch is the parliament, made up of two houses: the National Assembly and the Senate. The judicial branch consists of a system of courts. Power is thus separated into three branches as a system of checks and balances.

The National Assembly has 577 deputies elected by majority vote from the same number of single-seat constituencies for five-year terms. The 321 members of the Senate are indirectly elected by department electoral colleges from 108 multi-seat departments and territories for nine-year terms. The National Assembly is the more powerful of the two houses.

General Charles de Gaulle greatly increased the actual power of the president. As head of state, the president can dissolve the National Assembly and call for new elections at any time. In an emergency, the president can assume almost complete power.

LOCAL GOVERNMENT

France is divided into 22 decentralized *régions* ("RAY-giohn") for planning, budgetary policy, and national development. An earlier system, still in use, divided France into 96 *départements*. Each *département* has a main town and is run by a general council responsible for welfare, health, administration, and departmental employment services. It also has a commissioner representing the national government, and a local president.

The *départements* are divided into smaller units called *arrondissements* ("ah-rawn-diss-MAHN"). These are in turn subdivided into *cantons* ("KAHN-tohn") and *communes* ("koh-MUUH-nuh"). There are about 36,500 *communes* in France, ranging in size from small villages to entire cities. The *communes* are run by mayors elected by local municipal councils. One of the mayor's duties is to perform marriages.

In France there is a "political class" of men and women whose entire working lives are spent as professionals in government service.

Town halls range from the small functional office to striking architectural marvels such as the town hall of Paris.

POLITICAL PARTIES

It is thought that describing political parties as left- or right-wing stems from the French Revolution. Then, the radical reformers, the Jacobins, sat on the left side of the National Assembly, and the conservatives on the right.

Now many major political parties span the French spectrum from left-wing to right-wing. Parties on the left include the Socialist Party (PS), the smaller French Communist Party (PCF), and the populist Republican Pole (PR). On the right are the Union for French Democracy (UDF), the Union for the Presidential Majority (UMP), including Rally for the Republic (RPR) and Liberal Democracy (DL), and the conservative and xenophobic National Front (FN).

The leftist parties support public ownership or control of most industries but, in practice, have cooperated with private business since the 1930s. Both the socialists and communists support strong, government-financed social security and medical benefits. The rightist parties want less government regulation of the economy. The Rally for the Republic favors free enterprise but a strong national government and military, and an aggressive foreign policy. Labor unions and the Green Party, called *Les Verts* ("Lay Vayr"), also exert pressure on the government.

CRIME AND PUNISHMENT

French law cases are decided entirely on the basis of written law. French law is based on the constitution of the Fifth Republic, itself inspired by the Napoleonic Code. This means that besides the regular court system, there is a separate court system to deal specifically with legal problems of the French administration and its relation to the French citizen. A constitutional council rules on constitutional questions.

French *départements* have both civil and criminal courts, with Courts of Appeal for each. Cases involving murder and other serious offenses are heard in the Courts of Assizes. The highest court of the land is the Court of Cassation. Unlike the U.S. Supreme Court, it does not make a final decision. It can criticize legal proceedings and refer a case back to the lower courts to be reconsidered. In France, judges are appointed for life.

A famous image of French punishment has long been the guillotine. Originally used in Europe for executing criminals of noble birth, it was adopted during the French Revolution as a more humane, egalitarian, and quick way to execute a criminal, as compared with hanging, beheading, or quartering. The man whose name it bears, Dr. Joseph-Ignace Guillotin, was a physician and a member of the National Assembly. He influenced the passing of a law requiring all death sentences to be carried out using this decapitation machine, which he is said to have described as "a cool breath on the back of the neck." The guillotine has also been called "the national razor" and "the widow."

The French tend to be lenient about crimes of passion. When it is deemed that a normal person was driven by extreme emotion to commit murder, the penalty is less harsh. The guillotine was seldom used in the 20th century and last used in 1977. The death penalty was abolished in France in 1981.

Opposite: **The citizens of Paris frequently influence government policies by organizing mass demonstrations.**

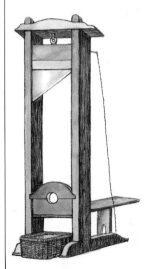

Above: **The guillotine was originally called louisette or louison before parliamentary correspondents named it after Dr. Guillotin.**

A distinctive feature of the French police is the *képi* ("keh-PEE"), the cap worn by police officers.

THE ARMED FORCES

The president of France heads its armed forces. About 2.5 percent of the country's gross domestic product (GDP) is spent on defense. Major reform of the armed forces was initiated in 1996 to professionalize the armed forces and eliminate the compulsory 10-month military service young Frenchmen had to serve. This was replaced in 2001 by a one-day session for all 17-year-old boys and girls to educate them on careers in the military. In 2002, 356,000 professional soldiers served in the army, navy, and air force. Volunteers between the ages of 18 and 30 also serve in the *gendarmerie* ("zhawn-DAHR-muh-REE") as militarized state police under the Minister of Defense, distinct from the National Police Force under the Minister of the Interior.

France has nuclear arms and is a major supplier of weapons. General Charles de Gaulle once said, "There is no corner of the earth where, at any given time, men do not look to us and ask what France has to say." This country's military and foreign policies do continue to affect the rest of the world.

The French Foreign Legion, staffed mainly by foreign volunteers, is part of a tradition of foreign troops who have served France since the Middle Ages. Formerly focused on French interests in Africa, it has increasingly become a peacekeeping force.

THE FRENCH FLAG

The French flag (*below*) is called the tricolor because it is divided into three equal vertical stripes of blue, white, and red. These colors were first used as a French emblem during the French Revolution. On July 17, 1789, King Louis XVI wore a tricolor knot of ribbons on his hat, combining the colors of Paris—red and blue—with white, the color of the royal family. France has no official coat of arms.

THE LEGION OF HONOR AND OTHER DECORATIONS

The highest French honor for outstanding military and civil service is the *Légion d'Honneur* ("Lay-JYOHN DON-er"), or Legion of Honor (*below*), created by Napoleon Bonaparte in 1802. During World War I, the *Croix de Guerre* ("KRWAH duh GEHR"), or Cross of War, commended bravery in battle, while the *Médaille Militaire (*"May-DIE meelee-TAIR"*)*, or Military Medal, was awarded to both combatants and noncombatants during World War I.

ECONOMY

FRANCE IS ONE OF the world's most highly developed economies. Modernization of French industry began in the early 1950s, and national policy has encouraged a tremendous growth in production and trade since World War II. Huge factories equipped with computers and machinery have replaced the typically small, prewar manufacturing enterprise. Many workers have left farms to staff the country's growing industrial centers.

France is among the world's top producers and consumers of nuclear power and offshore oil technology. It was the world's fourth largest industrial economy in 2001, when France's gross domestic product (GDP) was $1.2 trillion. Unemployment was 9.8 percent in 2002. The French government intervenes directly in the economy. Although this is slowly changing, the government still owns or partly owns many important industries to protect them from foreign competition.

Left: **The morning fruit market in Place Richelme, Aix-en-Provence. The Provençal markets are famous. Antibes, Grasse, Cannes, and Nice also have permanent markets selling fruit and vegetables, flowers, and local crafts. Weekly markets are also common in most French villages.**

Opposite: **Evian bottled water, distributed to more than 120 countries, originates as rain and snow in the French Alps. Over 15 years, water droplets make their way down to the spring at Evian-Les-Bains.**

Milking is done manually in small farms. France is famed for its dairy products, especially its wide variety of cheeses.

FERTILE SOIL

Of all France's natural resources, its soil is the most vital. A huge portion of French land is fertile, supporting crops such as wheat and sugar beets, fruit orchards, vineyards that generate the fabled wines of France, and grassland for grazing livestock. Agriculture, including fishing and forestry, used to be the backbone of the French economy but now accounts for only 3 percent of the GDP.

Acres of forests cover much of the French countryside. Their timber is used for buildings and making furniture and paper. Although forests are being destroyed at an alarming rate almost everywhere in the world, French forests are actually expanding as a result of careful government planning and reforestation.

The French have used their land resources wisely. The application of modern farming techniques, combined with government subsidies for farmers, have helped to make France a leading agricultural producer. Chief products, in addition to those already mentioned, include cattle, milk, potatoes, apples, hogs, and chickens. France grows most of its own food and also exports wheat and dairy products.

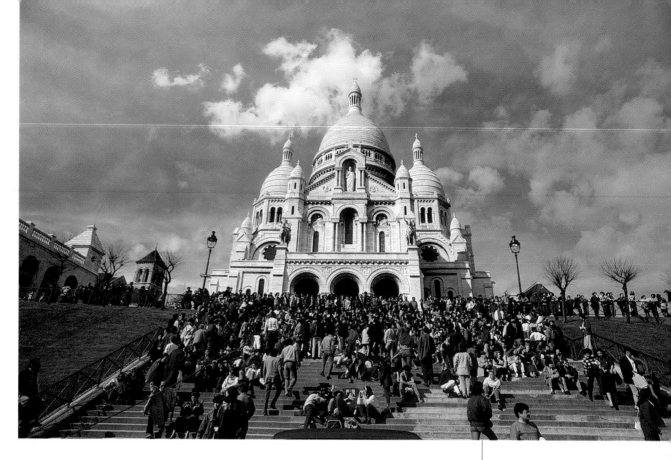

MINERALS

France has significant deposits of iron ore and bauxite (aluminum ore). The land also yields coal, gypsum, natural gas, petroleum, potash, salt, sulfur, tungsten, and zinc. France is a major producer of uranium, which is used for nuclear energy and weapons. French ores are used to produce aluminum and steel, essential materials for France's growing industries.

THE SERVICE INDUSTRIES

Seventy-one percent of the GDP comes from the service industries. In the past half century there has been a notable shift in employment away from agriculture and manufacturing into services. Seven out of every 10 French workers now work in industries such as education, health care, trade, banking, tourism, insurance, transportation, and communications. About 70 million tourists visited France in 1998. It is the third most-visited country in the world, after the United States and Italy. The French Club Méditerranée (Club Med) resort chain's annual revenue is about $2 billion.

The Sacré-Coeur in Paris attracts tourists all year round. France is one of the most popular tourist destinations in Europe. Tourism and travel brought in about $23.3 million in 1999.

The automobile industry is thriving in France. French-made cars are exported to many countries.

DESIGN AND MANUFACTURING

France is one of the most developed countries in the world, and industry accounts for 26 percent of France's GDP, with roughly one out of every four workers employed in industry. The diversified industrial sector includes electronics, food processing, metallurgy, mining, and the production of aircraft, automobiles, chemicals, machinery, steel, and textiles.

Products that the rest of the world associates France with are often luxury items, such as perfumes, gourmet foods and wines, and dyes and fine fabrics for the fashion industry. France also exports various high-technology products, such as the world's fastest trains, sophisticated electronic equipment, military airplanes and rockets, and communications satellites. Helicopter manufacturing and shipbuilding also continue to be important industries.

The automobile industry illustrates French talent for technical innovation and daring design. French engineers invented the clutch, gearbox, and transmission shaft and introduced the front-wheel drive system. Renault and PSA Peugeot Citroën are both among the top ten largest car manufacturers in the world.

Charming little shops in small towns or villages sell handmade glassware. The skill is handed down from parent to child.

French design talent has also contributed to the manufacture of aircraft such as the Caravelle commercial jet planes, the supersonic airliner Concorde, the internationally owned Airbus, and the Mystère and Mirage jet fighter planes. Arianespace, the world's leading launcher of commercial satellites, has its main offices located in Paris.

Quality and design are exemplified by Michelin tires, Chanel clothing and accessories, Limoges china, and hundreds of other products for which France is famous around the world.

Although Paris is the center of manufacturing, important factories dot many other regions of the country, and major centers have developed around the ports and coalfields. The metallurgical and textile industries have grown rapidly. More recently, the government has given cash and other incentives to promote new small factories in outlying regions.

A unique aspect of France is the survival of local artisanal traditions alongside industrialization. Particular products—gloves, glassware, lace, copper cookware, or knives, for example—are manufactured in towns or villages far from major industrial centers. These industries are based on locally available raw materials or skills passed down the generations.

Many factories using both nuclear and hydroelectric power have sprung up all over France.

ENERGY SOURCES

France's energy supplies are derived mainly from imported oil, coal, and natural gas, and domestic hydroelectricity and nuclear power.

Coalfields were exploited for hundreds of years until it became cheaper to import coal from abroad. Because of the shortage of coal reserves, hydraulic power has been harnessed where possible, such as at rivers and waterfalls in the Alps, Jura Mountains, Pyrenees Mountains, and the Massif Central.

France is one of the world's top producers of nuclear energy for electricity. Nuclear power plants supply about 75 percent of France's electricity.

The development of nuclear power plants in France stresses safety and economy, and thus nuclear power enjoys more popular support than in countries where serious nuclear accidents have occurred.

People's daily lives are affected by the French policy of energy conservation. The aim is to lessen French dependence on outside sources of power. Energy-saving plans include reduced speed limits for drivers and limits on home heating levels.

At the mouth of the Rance River on the coast of Brittany, a unique power plant converts the energy of the tides into electricity. Research on alternative power sources, such as solar power, continues.

TELECOMMUNICATIONS AND TRANSPORTATION

The French have an electronic communication system called *Minitel* that predates the Internet. More than 5.5 million telephone subscribers have a computer terminal in their home at no extra charge. They can use it to find numbers, make airplane and train reservations, order theater tickets, shop for goods and services, and "talk" via electronic mail. However, the French are increasingly turning to the Internet; some 8 million French privately connected to the Internet in 2001. Popular now are cable and Asymmetric Digital Subscriber Line (ADSL) high-speed Internet access for a permanent connection that does not depend on the phone line. French high schools are equipped with one computer for every six students.

Though the postal system is still owned and run by the French government, telephony and telecommunications have been privatized, with heavy competition between companies: France Telecom, Cégétel, and AT&T for fixed lines; Bouygues Télécom, SFR, and Itinéris for cellular phones; and AOL, Wanadoo, Club Internet, and Tiscali for Internet connections.

In 1981 the *Train à Grande Vitesse* ("Tran ah Grahnd Vee-tehss"), or TGV (*left*), literally High Speed Train, began running between Paris and Lyon. It now covers many destinations from Marseille in the south to Brussels in the north, Bordeaux in the southwest to Strasbourg in the east. The TGV is set to cover Turin and Milan in Italy, Barcelona in Spain, and Cologne and Frankfurt in Germany. The world speed record set by the TGV in 1990 was 320.3 miles (515.3 km) per hour, making it the fastest passenger train in the world. However, the average speed on daily runs is closer to 162 miles (261 km) per hour. The TGV *Eurostar* also uses the Eurotunnel, opened in 1994 under the British Channel, to reach London from Paris in a record time of three hours.

French commercial airlines include Air France, Air Inter, AOM, and Air Liberté.

France's 9,278 miles (14,932 km) of waterways transport heavy cargo, such as agricultural products, fuel, and raw materials. Paris is the most important riverport in France, followed by Strasbourg.

FOREIGN TRADE AND THE EUROPEAN UNION

France is the world's fourth largest exporter of goods (mainly durables) and ranks second in services and agriculture. It is the leading producer and exporter of farm products in Europe. Its major imports are petroleum products, machinery, agricultural products, chemicals, vehicles, aircraft, plastics, and iron and steel products. Major exports are machinery and transportation equipment, aircraft, plastics, pharmaceutical products, chemicals, agricultural products, iron and steel products, electronic and telecommunications equipment, textiles and clothing, and wines and brandies.

France invests tens of billions of dollars each year in foreign countries, especially former French colonies and other developing countries. France was a founding member of the European Economic Community (EEC) in 1958. Charles de Gaulle had envisioned the EEC as a world power bloc, inspired by France to remain independent of the United States and the Soviet Union. The EEC is now called the European Union (EU). Currently, France trades primarily with Germany, Spain, the United Kingdom, Italy, and the United States.

France participated in the 1992 Treaty of Maastricht, a project aiming to create a single economic area for Europe, to be on a more even economic footing with the United States. Member countries opened their frontiers and removed customs barriers and import taxes. Currency unity was attained for 300 million people when the euro replaced 12 different currencies in Europe on January 1, 2002, including the French franc. Further coordination in environment and education has been planned to strengthen the European economy. The success of the European Union will depend on cooperation among all its members. France, however, is also concerned to maintain its national autonomy and prestige.

FRENCH LUXURIES: PERFUME AND FASHION

The production of perfume has long been a major industry in France. French perfumes are exported to more than 100 countries.

Since the 1920s, famous fashion designers—Chanel, Yves St. Laurent, Christian Dior, Patou, and many others—have lent their names to perfumes and reaped fortunes.

Flowers grown in the south, especially around Grasse, have been used to make costly fragrances since the 16th century. Fields of lavender, carnations, lilies of the valley, and other flowers brighten the countryside around Grasse.

Today, plant oils, animal extracts, and less costly synthetic ingredients and chemicals are also prime ingredients in perfumes' closely guarded formulas. These formulas are tested by expert sniffers, mostly men, who are referred to in the business as "noses."

A second industry that links the name of France with elegance, style, quality, and luxury is the fashion industry. Other nations have looked to France for creative clothing designs since the 14th century.

In the mid-19th century, an Englishman, Charles Worth, founded the first couture house in Paris. Thus began the modern tradition of marketing fashion to wealthy women from many countries using beautiful models in seasonal fashion shows. New designs are quickly copied in less expensive versions.

French and foreign designers based in Paris influence the look of everything from ball gowns to sportswear, men's clothing, shoes, jewelry, and other accessories throughout the world. True believers in the power of French fashion claim that a silk scarf with the Hermès label can turn any outfit into the epitome of chic.

ENVIRONMENT

ECOLOGICAL AND ENVIRONMENTAL PROTECTION is a government priority and a major public concern in France. The Ministry for the Protection of Nature and the Environment was formed in 1971 with a mission to monitor the quality of the environment, protect nature, and prevent or reduce pollution. Starting in 1975, many laws were passed, and many public and semipublic environmental agencies set up.

NATIONAL PARKS

France has a rich flora of some 4,500 plants and is home to some 110 mammal, 360 bird, 30 amphibian, 36 reptile, and 72 fish species. Sadly, two animal species have become extinct and 24 are endangered, including the ibex, slender-billed curlew, Mediterranean monk seal, and Corsican red deer.

France started creating protected areas (now covering 7 percent of the total land area) in the 1960s. There are seven national parks in France, 40 regional nature parks, 149 natural reserves, and 299 protected coastal sites. These provide a haven for specific species of animals, birds, and fish. Human settlement and industry are forbidden in these areas. Regional nature conservation boards manage these protected areas in partnership with local authorities and private partners, buying or renting land to protect irreplaceable habitat areas.

The Pyrenees, with its breathtaking landscapes, lilies, chamois, griffon vultures, and astonishing midwife toads, is the most popular park. The Vanoise, Mercantour, and Ecrins national parks are located in the Alps; and the Cévennes National Park is south of the Massif Central. The Guadeloupe National Park extends over two islands: Grande-Terre and Basse-Terre. Port-Cros covers both land and sea: the islands of Port-Cros, Bagaud, Gabinière, and Rascas, and a 0.4-mile (600-m) marine belt around them.

49

CONSERVATION

The nature parks have been an important part of a tricky and ambitious conservation plan —to reintroduce next-to-extinct species in areas where they have almost disappeared.

Brown bears have been imported to populate the Pyrenees. In collaboration with neighboring Italy and Switzerland, lynx and hawks have been brought from Central Europe,

raised in captivity, and carefully released in the wild in the Alps. After years of effort and overcoming many unexpected difficulties, the organizers have brought a bear population of next to zero to a fragile but promising community of a dozen or more, just saving them from extinction in France.

The same initiative has been introduced for wolves in different areas, including Ardèche, with much less popularity among the farmers and neighbors, afraid for their cattle or for themselves.

Every spring, storks migrate back to Europe to nest and reproduce. It is common in Alsace to see huge nests on top of the chimneys of houses, and the owners are proud and considered lucky. Yet an extensive plan has been implemented to prepare suitable solid poles to welcome nests and to cover high-tension electrical power lines, where hundreds of young storks get killed every year.

One can also see bridges unconnected to roads and tiny tunnels in Picardy. They adorn highways in the middle of nowhere for the sole benefit of boars, deer, and hogs, who would get run over and crushed by cars if they crossed directly on the highway!

BLACK TIDES AND COASTAL PROTECTION

France has a powerful strategy to protect its coasts. Coastal land is purchased to protect it from urbanization, careless tourist projects, and industrial and domestic pollution. Authorities have had to act on a large scale several times in recent French history to clean hundreds of miles of beaches in Brittany from oil spilled from tankers.

The first devastating oil spill came from the *Torrey Canyon* in 1967, followed by the infamous *Amoco Cadiz* in 1978, and more recently the *Erika* in 1999. The *Erika* collapsed next to Belle-Île, an island off the southern coast of Brittany, and soiled 275 miles (440 km) of coastline. The *Amoco Cadiz* disaster, which spread 220,000 tons (220 million kg) of oil across 225 miles (360 km) of coastline around Portsall in the north of Brittany, killed or hurt 30,000 birds and destroyed one-fourth of all the region's oysters.

Sadly, many cargo ships still routinely pollute the shores by illegally cleaning their tanks in the open sea. Environmental teams and volunteers try to clean up the beach and animals affected by the spilled oil.

A little girl looks at a dead sea bird coated with crude oil. Groups of students from all over France spend their holidays supporting clean-up teams. Crude oil causes bird feathers to collapse and mat together, hampering the bird's ability to fly and keep warm. Birds also often ingest the toxic crude oil in an attempt to preen themselves and are poisoned.

A smoking landscape
after 180 firemen, 70
trucks, and three planes
suppressed the biggest
summer forest fire on
Corsica in 2002.

GROWING FORESTS

France has some of the largest forests in Europe: they cover some 25 percent of its territory. Observing that the Alpine, Pyrenean, and Massif Central environments were fragile and degraded, French officials in 1860 initiated an unprecedented policy of mountain reforestation. Today, France maintains this careful plan of reforestation to compensate for the industrial and agricultural use of wood, growing forests by around 1 percent annually. The program's major enemies: forest fires and fungus. Every summer the south of France and Corsica are ravaged by forest fires, destroying more than 173 square miles (448 square km) of forest annually.

Acid rain has given French forests a reddish tinge even in the greenest of springs. For most trees, there is no cure and they die slowly, unreplaced by new growth. At the end of 1999, severe storms destroyed forests and killed people in Europe, wiping out in a couple of nights what the French forestry industry would have consumed in nine months and disfiguring the landscape, including the historical gardens in the palace of Versailles.

POLLUTION

France has joined in most of the international agreements concerning industrial hazards and general pollution, including the Seveso rulings. These agreements cover the main polluters: quicksilver, lead, and cadmium, present in most industrial waste.

Asbestos, an insulation material widely used in buildings, has been found to cause cancer. The discovery that entire universities and schools were polluted with a cancer-causing substance raised a scandal. A wide-ranging program was implemented to remove the material and to protect students and workers from asbestos dust.

France has also subscribed to the Kyoto Protocol (1992), agreeing to limit greenhouse gas emissions. An air quality law was passed in 1996, but France fell short of the intended objectives, mainly because of the uncontrolled rise in car usage. To fight this problem, the government is trying to promote public transportation across France. One initiative is car-free days, created in 1998 and involving 66 cities by 1999. People are urged to leave their cars at home on car-free days and use public transportation or bicycles.

KEEPING THE WATER CLEAN

France's water reserves are abundant but unequally distributed. Six regional agencies control the use and safety of water supplies. Some mineral water companies, such as Evian, Vichy, and Perrier, are under scrutiny. France introduced the "who pollutes pays" rule to finance the protection and cleaning of its used water. The main dangers to clean water come from the abusive use of chemical fertilizers, the illegal dumping of industrial waste, and the growing needs of the population.

The biggest consumer of water remains the state-owned Electricité de France (EDF), the French power agency, and its dam and power plant projects. Dams encounter a lot of resistance from ecologists who worry about industrial pollution and fear for the ecosystems of these rivers.

FOOD SAFETY

Food security is no longer an issue in Europe, but food safety has become a major concern. Mad cow disease is one striking example. The scare first started in Britain in 1996. Measures have been taken in France to slaughter all sick animals and forbid the sale and import of contaminated meat, from the United Kingdom in particular.

A strict and comprehensive monitoring structure has been put in place to control cultivation, preparation, and storage to ensure the wholesomeness of French food. More and more farmers have switched to biological agriculture, and bio-labels have been created to ensure that products called "bio" are free of chemical fertilizers.

Ecologists in France have a widespread mistrust of genetically modified plants. They contend that cultivation of these plants upsets the ecological balance and that eating them may prove dangerous. They want strong regulation and scientific monitoring to ensure that all risks are understood and analyzed.

WASTE DISPOSAL

Each year French households produce over 24 million tons (24 trillion kg) of waste, more than double the amount 30 years ago. This means that each person generates an average of 0.4 tons (416 kg) of waste each year.

Streamlining French waste management through waste recovery and making waste financially self-supporting is foremost in the minds of French authorities, with some success. Some 55 percent of glass and 45 percent of paper used is recycled. Each city has a specific plan for selective waste disposal: for glass, paper, plastic, and dangerous items such as batteries, printer cartridges that contain lead, car fuel, and car batteries. Waste collection, treatment, and disposal is a growing business in France.

NUCLEAR ENERGY

France made the strategic choice to develop nuclear power in the 1970s, and 50 percent of French energy consumption is met this way. France is the second in the world, after the United States, in nuclear development. As an active nuclear power, France conducted experimental nuclear tests in French Polynesia for several years that raised worldwide protests.

Nuclear power does not pollute the air or aggravate the greenhouse effect, but uranium is one of the trickiest substances to handle and must be safely stored for thousand of years. In 1986 fears became reality when the Chernobyl nuclear plant in the USSR burned, sending a huge radioactive cloud into the air. When the cloud drifted over France, government authorities advised against eating fresh products for a while. With time, the danger seems to have subsided. The Chernobyl incident raised many doubts about the use of nuclear energy, and France is now exploring alternative non-polluting energies, such as solar and wind power and energy recycling.

A wind farm in France. France still lags behind other European nations in its investment in wind power.

THE FUTURE

Unlike the United States, France does not have a specific organization devoted to environmental research. Nevertheless, France has registered 12 percent of the world patents for environmental technologies.

The ecologists have a specific political party, called *Les Verts*, or The Greens, which aims to play a bigger role in major issues such as water safety, industrial waste control, education, and raising awareness about environmental issues among the general population.

THE FRENCH

ALTHOUGH AROUND 60 MILLION PEOPLE live in France, the country is so large that it has a relatively low population density (about 277 people per square mile, or 107 per square km) when compared to other countries in Europe. In addition, the overseas departments and territories are home to about 2 million people.

French people are quite varied in appearance, reflecting the country's history as a crossroads of Europe. Early in its history, the region of France was already a melting pot of many tribes: Mediterranean, Alpine, and Nordic. The Celtic, Teutonic, Slavic, and Viking tribes brought with them different physical traits and customs.

In the mid-19th century, the need for workers brought an influx of immigrants from Belgium, Italy, and Poland. After World War I, immigrants arrived from Algeria, Italy, Portugal, and Spain. Between 1956 and 1976, large numbers of Arabs and Jews left North Africa to settle in France.

Stereotypes abound. People expect the French from the north to be tall, blond, and blue-eyed. Northerners are sometimes perceived as more sophisticated than their southern neighbors, who are expected to be shorter, olive-skinned, dark-eyed, more easygoing, and slower-paced.

Above: **Farmers all over the country sport a tanned and rugged look.**

Opposite: **Celebrations for a wine festival in Beaune. The French always enjoy a party.**

Such generalizations about the French quickly break down. The French are mobile within their borders, like many other populations. Large numbers have moved from village to city and from north to south in the pursuit of jobs and better lifestyles. In addition, 12 percent of the French own second homes (a world record), often in regions far removed from their primary household, giving them roots in more than one region of the country.

Still, the diverse French people appear somewhat homogeneous to outsiders. Perhaps what unifies them is the French language and the strong influence exerted by Paris over the rest of the country. Most French people also share the unifying link of their unique history and culture, combined with a fierce love for their country.

Writer Christopher Sinclair-Stevenson in his book *When in France* observed: "The French are grumblers, but on one point they are united: France is, for all her faults, the best, most civilized, most beautiful country in the world."

CITY AND COUNTRY FOLK

France has at least 57 cities and towns with more than 100,000 people. The largest cities are Paris, Lyon, Marseille, Lille, Bordeaux, Toulouse, and Nice. During the postwar urbanization of France, Paris doubled in size, while the university town of Grenoble grew rapidly from 80,000 people to more than 405,000. About 74 percent of the population now live in cities and towns, with the remaining 26 percent in rural areas.

About one-sixth of the total French population live in greater metropolitan Paris. Paris is the developed world's most densely populated major city. The first Parisians were a tribe of Gauls called the Parisii, who settled an island in the Seine River known as Île de la Cité. The majority of Parisians have moved out of Paris to live in the suburbs.

Above: **Mediterranean-looking French, with dark hair and an olive complexion, are no longer confined to the south but are seen everywhere in France.**

Opposite: **Cellular phones and motorbikes are trendy in France, as in other parts of the world.**

58

Today, Paris is the capital of French government, business, and culture. It sets the trends for the rest of the country in fashion, intellectual life, and the arts. It is also one of the most beautiful cities in the world, with elegant restaurants and shops, famous museums and monuments, churches, plazas, boulevards, gardens and parks, and the picturesque Seine River. Paris is the home of many rich individuals, both French and foreign. Efficient but less attractive modern developments surround the city to house its expanding population.

Centers of population grew either to meet the demands of industry and trade or because of the amenities of resort areas, such as those along the Mediterranean Sea and in the warm, sunny towns in southern France. Most large cities are located near water: on the coast or along inland waterways.

Since the end of World War II, masses of villagers, especially young people, have moved to urban areas in search of better job opportunities and a more comfortable lifestyle. Some villages in poorer regions of the country are now almost deserted.

A recent counter-trend has found young people moving back to the countryside to enjoy and protect France's natural environment, run small businesses, and produce crafts.

A large number of French people belong to the *petite bourgeoisie*. They hold jobs in offices, such as in banks, and are generally quite well off.

SOCIAL CLASSES

Although the feudal days of the monarchy and nobility are long past, social classes remain. The aristocracy maintains its inherited titles and property, and many members of the aristocracy live in elegant country chateaus and Parisian apartments. However, this class no longer dominates the country as it once did. Increasingly, members of the old aristocracy have intermarried with wealthy members of the middle class.

France has a large middle class, or bourgeoisie, that virtually runs the country. This class dominates the elite schools and universities. They are doctors, lawyers, teachers, bankers, and industrialists as well as sales executives, skilled technicians, newly rich merchants, and foreign-service professionals. Many leading politicians come from this class. The wealthier and more powerful members of the bourgeoisie make up about 15 percent of the labor force. A larger group (about 40 percent of the labor force), called the petite bourgeoisie, includes people in small- and medium-sized businesses, artists and intellectuals, and many office workers.

STRONG REGIONAL IDENTITIES

Regional variations in appearance and customs are most noticeable near the country's borders where certain subgroups of the French population retain distinctive customs, languages, attitudes, and even styles of dress that set them apart.

The people of Brittany, Bretons, express a strong individuality bearing the stamp of their Celtic origins. Regional pride has led many Bretons to retain their ancient language and folk festivals and dress.

The French of Alsace share favorite food such as sauerkraut with their German neighbors. Alsatians drink more beer than wine and speak a dialect mixed with German.

In southern France, many people in Provence have retained a Provençal dialect influenced by their Roman heritage. The 100,000 Basques have a language unrelated to other European tongues and a unique heritage of folklore.

Like Bretons, the people of Corsica have a strong regional identity. Corsican separatists have begun to achieve their goals in seeking independence from France.

The working class includes farmers, makers of goods, and manual workers—some 45 percent of the labor force. This class may share lifestyle patterns with the middle class, but they do not advance through the state schools with the same degree of success. In spite of France's ideals of equality, only about 9 percent of university students come from the working class. A major gap between rich and poor still exists.

More conducive to the ideal of equality is the social welfare system. Rich and poor share equitably in such benefits as maternity care, bonuses for having children, day care for young children, general health and dental care, disability assistance, and retirement pensions. Around 16 percent of the population are age 65 or older, which places a financial burden on workers to help support those who are retired.

France enjoys a low infant mortality rate, and the average life span is 75 years for men and 83 for women. In 2001 the population growth was 0.37 percent and the total fertility rate 1.75 children born per woman.

IMMIGRANTS' INFLUENCE ON FRENCH LIFE

Immigration has added to the diversity of the French population, at times raising troubling questions about French identity and sparking social tensions. Many famous French citizens, from designer Pierre Cardin to actor Yves Montand, had foreign parents.

Since the 1850s, there has been a steady flow of immigrants into France. Now about 9 percent of the French population are immigrants. In the period between the World Wars, France needed manpower and opened its doors to job-seekers, such as Italians and Poles, and refugees, such as Greeks, Armenians, Russians, and Spaniards. After World War II, immigrants (mainly young men) from Italy, Spain, Portugal, sub-Saharan Africa, the Middle East, and Asia arrived to aid France in its 30-year period of high economic growth. A rise in unemployment in the 1970s led to measures to curb immigration. There was a drop in immigration, and it consisted more of women and children reuniting with their families in France. About 800,000 French citizens returned from Algeria when it gained independence in 1962. Hundreds of thousands of immigrants have sought political refuge in France in recent years: Chileans, Iranians, Palestinians, Poles, and Vietnamese; and others from Latin America, Eastern Europe, and Russia. Illegal immigration has become a problem.

Large groups of immigrants live in Paris and its environs and in the regions of the Rhône-Alps, Provence, and the Riviera. Large settlements of Muslims are concentrated in the port city of Marseille.

France's ultraright National Front Party, headed by Jean-Marie Le Pen, has responded to these new arrivals by encouraging racial intolerance. To counter that influence, a group of students formed SOS Racisme with the slogan *"Ne touche pas à mon pote!"* ("neu TOOSH pah ah mohn POT"), meaning "Don't touch my buddy!"

WHAT IS SO FRENCH ABOUT THE FRENCH?

The French exemplify strong individualism, value family life, and defend dearly what they consider their collective rights. They love life and the finer things in it, from food and wine to the arts. Many French people enjoy engaging in long and passionate conversations on any number of topics, in public or private settings. They share a conservative respect for tradition and a reverence for the past. French family ties are strong and most parents live close to their grown children, often taking an active role in raising their grandchildren.

The French take great pride in French products and French style. Many believe in preserving the purity of their beautiful language, going to great lengths to limit the import of foreign words into the daily vocabulary.

French people generally like order but hate to be disciplined; they admire logic, cleverness, and wit. They think they are different from the rest of the world, often to the point where they believe foreigners cannot understand them.

On closer inspection, images of the French are varied and often contradictory. From peasant to aristocrat, the French are like their food—full of flavor and rarely dull.

French men and women carry themselves with an indefinable air of confidence and style.

LIFESTYLE

THE FRENCH PEOPLE have varied customs and traditions. City life is not the same as country life, and different social classes behave differently. But *joie de vivre* ("JWAH duh VE-vruh"), a joy in living, is an essential element of every French lifestyle. And savoir-faire, the ability to say and do the right thing in any situation, is one of the graces French parents hope to pass on to their children.

FAMILY TIES

The French cherish family ties. The family is a working unit, a community of interests, leisure pursuits, and affection.

Depending on income and social circumstances, different rates of child benefit, childcare allowances, and student accommodation grants can be claimed by around 10 million French families. These claims are handled by the Caisse d' Allocation Familiale (CAF), or Family Allowance Office, which has about 20,000 employees.

In earlier times, a large extended family of grandparents, parents, and children all lived together in one household. Today, as customs have changed and the birth rate is relatively low (around 12 births per 1,000

people), a typical family is smaller—just the parents and one to three children. Many children live at home and go to a school or a university near their home. When they marry, French couples tend to settle not farther than about 10 miles (16 km) away from their childhood homes.

65

CITY LIFESTYLE

The pace of life in cities, especially in Paris, is faster and more hectic than in the countryside. Traffic in the city center is more congested, and the sheer size of the population sometimes makes people more irritable. In the larger cities most people live in small apartments. The older buildings are often considered more attractive, with their handsome carved moldings and working fireplaces.

Many young people own a motorbike that they ride to school or to meet friends. Groups of teenagers on bikes near cafés or sidewalks are a common sight.

Zoning laws protect the environment of most French city centers, of which there are about 20, limiting building size and regulating traffic. Few buildings in French city centers rise higher than eight or nine floors. Rows of trees line the sides of main avenues, and flowers brighten the squares and central strips along main streets. Thousands of workers in green uniforms sweep the streets, keeping them clean.

In the cities, sidewalk cafés are one of the pivots of daily life. People linger here, sipping a cup of coffee or a glass of wine, watching the world pass by. Café owners encourage patrons to stay as long as they wish. Famous writers Jean-Paul Sartre and Simone de Beauvoir wrote their books in a café on the Parisian Left Bank, the traditional heart of French intellectual, bohemian, and political life.

Cafés attract mainly writers, artists, musicians, and students. Young people flirt and play jukeboxes and pinball machines in cafés. They also spend their free time in discos and shopping malls.

City streets are generally named after famous people, trades and professions, historical events, or artists. These names often change with changes in politics.

Paris is France's romantic capital city and receives tens of thousands of tourists annually. It is divided into 20 *arrondissements* ("AH-rohn-DISS-mohn"), or districts.

Surrounding the cities are burgeoning suburbs, often with massive government housing developments where poorer people can afford to live. More than half the urban population live in new suburban houses or apartment buildings. Suburbanites commute to work on mass transit systems, such as the *Métro* in Paris, and other modes of public transportation.

Some city dwellers feel that their housing is overcrowded and unhealthy. The richer suburbs are pleasant, but the poorer ones can be quite grim and rife with crime and racism. Those who can afford it escape to a second home in the country on weekends or vacations. Many have converted old farmhouses, deserted by previous owners who have moved to the city.

People in the cities tend to view country people as old-fashioned, stubbornly adhering to old habits, customs, values, and beliefs. On the other hand, they admire country people as the embodiment of hard work, individualism, frugality, and common sense. There is a growing nostalgia for the land and the way of life it represents.

The French, particularly young urbanites, are increasingly influenced by trends of modernization and "Americanization." They enjoy hamburgers, American movies, television programs, and popular music. They love to wear American blue jeans, athletic shoes, and baseball jackets and caps.

"It is hard to find a city-dweller in France who has not somewhere in the provinces a parcel of land to which he is strongly attached and to which, very often, it is his dream at last to retire. There is a peasant beneath the surface of every urban Frenchman. ..."

—*Waverley Root, 20th-century writer.*

The café is the meeting place for country folk. Here they spend long hours catching up on gossip or discussing politics and current affairs.

RURAL LIFESTYLE

Many rural towns look almost the same as they did hundreds of years ago. In the heart of town is a square bordered by a church, and small stores and cafés. Old men play *boules* ("BOO-luh"), or lawn bowling, while others chat and gossip. They sit in the cafés, eating and drinking, reading, writing, or playing chess.

Typical shops include the bakery, the butcher's, and the *charcuterie* ("shar-koo-tuh-REE"), a type of delicatessen selling cooked meats and sausages. The *tabac* ("tah-BAHK") sells stamps, newspapers, and cigarettes. Other small stores sell fresh fish, groceries, and medicines.

Most rural people live in single-story dwellings. Their stone houses have brown, gray, or green wooden shutters. Villagers usually own a car, a television, and modern household appliances.

A typical village will have a belfry tower, a small post office, a café, one or two restaurants, a town hall with the French flag flying, and an elementary school. Many towns have a weekly outdoor market selling fresh produce and sometimes live chickens and rabbits.

Many people in the countryside are farmers or work in small businesses and have never traveled far from their villages. Some still live in homes with dirt floors and no indoor plumbing, maintaining a centuries-old way of life. But French society continues to modernize, the image of old peasant villagers slowly being replaced by that of modern business people.

The French education system is based on discipline and innovation. Students are expected to work hard and participate actively in class.

EDUCATION

French schools must be doing something right because an impressive 99 percent of the population aged 15 and above can read and write.

Education is provided free by the government and is compulsory for children between the ages of 6 and 16. The Ministry of National Education designs the curriculum and the examinations that students must pass. Children between the ages of 2 and 6 may attend nursery schools and kindergartens funded by the government. Reading is taught from age 5 onward.

Government schools are secular. French families can also choose to send their children to privately run religious schools. These schools are mostly Roman Catholic, but some are Protestant or Jewish. A law from 1959 allows private establishments to sign contracts to receive state funds in exchange for some state control. About 15 percent of French children attend private elementary schools, rising to about 23 percent at the secondary level.

French schools are highly competitive, expecting students to master a wide range of subjects. Discipline tends to be quite strict. In France, as elsewhere in the world, the teaching of computer skills is well-integrated into the curriculum.

SORBONNE UNIVERSITY

The Sorbonne is one of the oldest universities in Paris, founded by the theologian Robert de Sorbon around 1257. Teaching at the university had become secular since the late 19th century. In May 1968 a protest initiated at the Sorbonne led to nation-wide educational reform.

The Sorbonne is now one of the most famous institutions of higher learning in the world. It has outgrown its original home on the Left Bank and has expanded to 13 separate campuses.

Little time is devoted to after-school activities or interschool sports competitions. French children have a very long school day (from 9 A.M. to 4:30 P.M. with an hour and a half for lunch) and usually two hours of daily homework, but they enjoy a long school vacation—about three months a year. Wednesday is a free day when schoolchildren can pursue games or cultural activities such as art, music, or dance, but students must attend school on Saturday morning.

Secondary school consists of four years of *collège* ("koh-LEHZH") and three years of *lycée* ("lee-SAY"), beginning at around age 11. After *collège*, some students continue their education at a vocational *lycée* to prepare for a job. Students with better grades fulfill the three years of general *lycée* to prepare for the baccalaureate exam, which they take when they are 18 or older. This exam is so difficult that roughly one-third of the students who take it fail.

Successful candidates for the baccalaureate receive free university education or attend one of the famous *grandes écoles*, elite colleges that train students for the top careers in government service, business, mathematics, and engineering.

The *grande école* L'Ecole Nationale d'Administration (ENA) has been called the most exclusive and prestigious school in France. Its students are almost certain that their intense study for two and a half years will lead them to the top in government or politics.

Military academies prepare students for military careers. Family tradition is strong here—eight out of 10 students in these schools are children of active officers in the French armed forces.

FRENCHWOMEN

Frenchwomen are perceived to be beautifully dressed and alluring. They are often efficient housewives who spend money carefully. In many small family businesses, the women control the cash.

Frenchwomen did not vote until 1945. Up to 1965 the husband was the legal head of the family, and the wife needed her husband's permission to get a job or a passport. The husband managed his wife's money and bank account.

Frenchwomen today are achieving more equality. Birth control became available in 1967, and in 1975 abortion and divorce by mutual consent were legalized.

Today women are competing with men for prestigious positions in the corporate world. Although the law guarantees women equal pay, Frenchwomen's average salaries are still far below those of Frenchmen.

Women have long been influential in the French labor movement. As a group, they are taking an increasing interest in politics. They have been elected to parliament and to municipal councils. In 1991 Edith Cresson became the first woman prime minister of France.

Today's Frenchwoman is a free spirit who is still fighting to gain equality with men in the workplace.

FRENCH CUSTOMS AND MANNERS

The French shake hands when greeting friends and saying goodbye. Close friends and relatives greet one another with a kiss on each cheek, some southerners adding a third kiss. When a French person enters a room on a social occasion, the newcomer greets everyone in the room. Traditionally, people call only close friends by their first names, although young people are often more informal about using first names.

The French rarely visit someone's home without an invitation. Invitations are usually answered in writing, and thank-you notes are sent soon after a party. Families enjoy sharing meals together. They gather around the table to feast together during holidays and important family events. Children generally remain out of sight when their parents have dinner parties at home. Popular gifts to bring to a dinner party are a box of candy, cookies, or an odd number of flowers. But a visitor should never bring chrysanthemums, which are associated with funerals. The French do not like to discuss business during social meals.

French customs and manners

The French address people as *Monsieur* ("muh-SYER"), meaning Mr. or Sir; *Madame* ("mah-DAHM"), meaning Mrs., Madam, or Ma'am; and *Mademoiselle* ("mahd-mwah-ZEHL"), meaning Miss or young lady. They use these titles far more often than English-speaking people do, and they use them generally without adding the person's name: "*Bonjour* ("bawn-ZHOOR"), *Monsieur*" instead of "Hello, Mr. Jones." The second person singular *tu/toi* is reserved for close friends and family members of the same age or younger. The more formal second person form, *vous*, is used when speaking to superiors.

Some topics are not considered appropriate for polite conversation: people's age, income, occupation, and questions about their family such as how many brothers and sisters they have. Asking how much a personal possession costs or where it was bought is also considered rude, as are talking loudly, chewing gum in public, and calling attention to oneself.

It is sometimes said that the French are careful with money, love a bargain, and try to pay as few taxes as possible to the government. Those who dream of becoming instant millionaires may bet at the horse races or buy National Lottery (*Loto*) tickets at the corner kiosk.

The French love to argue and debate, criticize and complain, and they express their true feelings with a gusto that might seem rude to people from other cultures. They tend to be highly critical of both government and business. Although not a nation of "joiners," they sometimes get together for group protests, which occasionally grow into riots or strikes.

The young can be particularly restless, as was illustrated in the student-worker Paris Riots of 1968. Yet there is also in the French people a strong conservative streak that resists change.

French compassion for needy people throughout the world is seen in French volunteer groups such as Médecins Sans Frontières ("made-SAN sahn fron-TEEAYR"), or Doctors without Borders.

p74: **Almost half of all Frenchwomen work outside the home, especially in the textile, retail, and other service industries.**

WORK AND TRAVEL

The French business day begins at around 9 A.M. and ends at 6 P.M. People work Monday to Friday and are expected to be prompt for appointments. Department stores are usually closed on Sunday and Monday. Most offices and shops close from noon to 2 P.M. Fathers and children used to come home for lunch, but with more mothers working, this practice is growing less common.

French workers are entitled to five weeks of vacation a year, and many divide this into three weeks of summer vacation in the month of August and two in the winter.

French cities generally have a cheap and dependable bus service, and comfortable trains cross the country. The Paris subway system, the *Métro*, is one of the most efficient in the world. On buses and subways, people often give up their seats to senior citizens.

Getting around in cars is somewhat more hazardous, as the French tend to drive faster than official speed limits. Children are required to ride in the back seat of cars. By law, every passenger in a car must wear a seat belt. It is illegal to honk the car horn in a town. Young people can ride motorized two-wheel mopeds from the age of 14.

THE FRENCH LOVE THEIR DOGS

The well-dressed Frenchwoman dining in an elegant restaurant with a French poodle on her lap reflects the national passion for pet dogs. One French home in three has a dog. People walking in Paris reportedly step in dog droppings every 286th step! It is the city council that cleans up the mess, not the owners.

French thinker Blaise Pascal wrote in the 17th century: "The more I see of man, the more I love my dog." Dogs symbolizing faithfulness were carved on the tombs of French queens. Hunters, including French kings and noblemen, have long idolized their hounds. Napoleon had a favorite poodle named Moustache.

Along with pigs, French dogs, especially poodles, are used to sniff out the valuable underground truffles so highly prized in French cooking. (Unlike pigs, dogs can be trusted not to swallow the truffles.)

German shepherds, wirehaired dachshunds, Yorkshire terriers, and red cocker spaniels are among the most popular breeds with French pet owners. French dogs are often named for opera characters and figures in ancient history; common names include Rex, Fifi, Loulou, Princesse, and Whisky. The name Toutou is either supposed to sound like barking or stems from the word *tu*, the familiar form of the word "you," used to address children.

On the outskirts of Paris, there is a private cemetery for dogs, the first in the world. Built at the end of the 19th century, it is the final resting place for the pets of both world-famous and unknown French doglovers.

75

RELIGION

FOR MUCH OF FRENCH HISTORY, religious differences have sparked conflicts and bloody wars.

Most French are Roman Catholic. Roman Catholicism inspired the magnificent churches and cathedrals that are found in many parts of France. In 1789 the state ceased to be officially Catholic. Napoleon's Concordat of 1801 recognized the Catholic Church as the religion of the majority, and Protestants were given freedom of worship. In 1905 a law was passed clearly separating church and state. All citizens were guaranteed freedom of religious belief and practice.

The French government is neutral in religious matters and tolerates the peaceful coexistence of different religious groups.

Left: **Although fewer French people today believe in the existence of God, religious fervor is still strong among the millions of believers. Religious instruction, however, is expressly forbidden in state schools.**

Opposite: **The Cathedral de Notre Dame is one of the most enduring symbols of Paris.**

THE ROMAN CATHOLIC CHURCH TODAY

About 90 percent of French people consider themselves Roman Catholic, and most have been baptized. But only about 14 percent attend church regularly. Some sections of the country have a much higher percentage of practicing Catholics than others—up to 80 percent in those rural areas where religious traditions are strongest. Devout Catholics make pilgrimages to holy sites such as Lourdes, where the Virgin Mary is believed to have appeared in a vision.

First Holy Communion is an important step in a Catholic's life. For the ceremony, both boys and girls dress in white and girls wear a veil.

People who rarely go to church may attend Mass during major events in their lives. Almost all Catholics are baptized, married, and buried by the Church. After a christening, guests and children near the church receive blue or pink candy-coated almonds called *dragées* ("drah-ZHAY"). A special ceremony is held when children first receive Holy Communion and Confirmation at around age 11 or 12. They may be given a gift, wrapped in white. First Holy Communion is celebrated with a special lunch attended by the whole family. Only white food, such as chicken and white asparagus, is served.

The Roman Catholic Church has its own school system, newspapers, social service organizations, and youth groups. Critics of the French Roman Catholic Church claim that it is rigid, traditional, and distant.

The influence of the Church on the French people has diminished greatly. Fewer men now choose to become priests, and many people ignore Church doctrine forbidding divorce, abortion, and birth control.

Recognizing a need for change, the Church has tried to reach out to more people, adapting to the needs of modern lifestyles without losing the traditions of the past. Prayer services were simplified in the 1960s, and Masses are now conducted in French rather than in Latin.

The Church has stepped up its involvement in progressive social action. Some worker-priests hold ordinary jobs and try to share the lives of the working class. An ecumenical outreach to non-Catholic Christians and to people of other religions marks the current attitude of the Catholic Church in France and the world.

Some conservative Church leaders, led by the far-right former archbishop Monseigneur Lefebvre, have reacted strongly against these liberalizing trends in the Church. About 10 percent of Catholics support a return to old-fashioned discipline and strict observance of doctrine.

MIRACLE AT LOURDES

Devout Roman Catholics make pilgrimages to sites where they believe miracles have occurred. One much-visited shrine is in Lourdes in southwestern France. There, in 1858, Bernadette Soubirous, a sick 14-year-old girl from a poor family, said that the Virgin Mary had appeared to her. Altogether, Bernadette had 18 visions. In the grotto where she said she had seen the Virgin, Bernadette had scratched the dry ground with her fingers and water had flowed out where no spring had existed before. The water appeared to have healing powers, and, even a century and a half after, millions of people bathe in the water with hopes of being cured of their illnesses.

Church officials were initially skeptical, but decades later, after much inquiry, Rome declared the events at Lourdes miraculous. In 1933, 54 years after Bernadette's death at the age of 35, the Church canonized her a saint. The world's largest underground church, capable of seating 20,000 to 30,000 people, was built to mark the 100th anniversary of the miracle.

Around 6 million pilgrims visit Lourdes each year, with the largest of six yearly pilgrimages on August 15 (Assumption Day). People light candles and kneel to express their faith. They pray to the Virgin to cure their illnesses and disabilities. Discarded crutches are stacked at the entrance to the Cave of Apparitions.

The health of the local economy also benefits from the miracle. Lourdes has the largest number of hotel rooms of any French city except Paris. Souvenir shops sell plastic bottles in the shape of the Virgin, filled with holy water from the spring.

PROTESTANTS IN FRANCE

Protestants, called Huguenots in France, were once spread throughout the country, but the 16th-century Wars of Religion and the revocation of the Edict of Nantes in 1685 greatly reduced their presence. Many children born to Protestant parents did not have any civil status because Roman Catholic priests, the only ones authorized to conduct marriage services, refused to officiate at Protestant weddings. It was not until 1787 that the Promulgation of the Edict of Toleration partially restored the civil and religious rights of Protestants. Freedom of worship was eventually granted during the French Revolution.

A major French Protestant reformer was John Calvin (1509–64). He was educated in law and theology. *Institutes of the Christian Religion* was his masterpiece, an important statement of Protestant belief. Calvin believed that human beings cannot save themselves from their sins, that only God can free them. He also believed in the Bible as the sole authority for the Christian faith.

Today, about 2 percent of the French are Protestant, belonging to several different denominations. The leading one is the Reformed Church of France. Activities of all the Protestant churches are coordinated by the Protestant Federation of France. Protestants live in areas such as Paris, Alsace, the Jura Mountains, and the Massif Central. They are active in French business and politics, with at least five appointed prime minister.

On the night of August 24, 1572, thousands of Protestants were massacred in Paris, sparking off the Wars of Religion.

OTHER RELIGIONS

With about 2 million believers, Islam is the second largest religion in France, after Roman Catholicism. The Muslim population includes many recent immigrants from North Africa. Muslims have settled especially in Marseille and the immigrant neighborhoods of Paris.

There are more Jews living in France than in any other Western European country. About 1 percent of the French people are Jewish. They live in and around Paris, in Marseille, and in the larger towns in the eastern regions.

Anti-Semitic sentiments in the seventh and 14th centuries led to the expulsion of thousands of French Jews. Later, they endured deportation to the death camps during World War II when France was occupied by Nazi Germany.

France imposed heavy penalties for racist, antisemitic, and xenophobic acts following attacks in the early 1990s by the extreme right-wing National Front Party and neo-Nazi groups on both the Muslim and Jewish communities and their mosques or synagogues, businesses, and cemeteries.

Jewish life thrives, marked by flourishing kosher restaurants, Hebrew schools, and synagogues. Jewish children are usually given names of Catholic saints, although their last names often reveal their heritage.

Small immigrant groups also practice Hinduism, Buddhism, and other religions. Newer groups such as the Moonies and Hare Krishna have not gained a large following. Freemasons have a long history in France. They participate actively in politics, with a tendency toward leftist views. About 4 percent of the French declare themselves unaffiliated to any religion.

Opposite: **Islam is the fastest-growing religion in France, practiced by many North African immigrants.**

RELIGION INFLUENCES FIRST NAMES

Since 1539 parents have been legally required to register their children's names. Until the Revolution, babies had to be named after a Roman Catholic saint.

In addition to birthday celebrations, the French people sometimes also have a party on their Name Day, the feast day of the saint after whom they are named. Even non-Catholics tend to give their children the first names of Catholic saints.

With certain exceptions, French citizens cannot legally change their names as registered at birth.

Popular first names include Jean, Pierre, Jacques, André, Claude, Michel, and Pierre for boys, and Marie, Jeanne, Françoise, Monique, Brigitte, Martine, and Sylvie for girls. Double first names, such as Jean-Pierre or Marie-Christine, are also a popular practice. Young modern parents are now picking names such as Lucas, Thomas, Hugo, and Théo for boys, and Camille, Manon, Chloé, and Léa for girls.

LANGUAGE

ONE OF THE JEWELS OF FRANCE is its official language, French. This precise and beautiful tongue has been a major factor unifying the diverse peoples of France and an ambassador for French culture around the world.

A LANGUAGE OF CLARITY AND BEAUTY

Many past European intellectuals and leaders have preferred French to their native tongues. French has thrived as a language of diplomacy and is today the only language other than English in which United Nations documents are published.

French is the official language of more than 25 countries, including Belgium, Canada, French Guiana, Haiti, Luxembourg, Monaco, and Switzerland. It is also used by French overseas *départements* and in many former French colonies. More than 112 million people around the world speak French as their first language, and millions more speak it as a second language.

Below: **Drama practice in the park. The French are very proud of their language, which is perceived as a language of refinement.**

Opposite: **A French newspaper vendor is almost hidden by his wares.**

The governments of French-speaking countries created an organization in 1986 called the *Organisation Internationale de La Francophonie.* Its members wrestle with world problems, agriculture, scientific research, and other areas of mutual concern. The University Agency of Francophonie was founded in Montreal in 1961 to develop the exchanges and solidarity among universities teaching French.

SOURCES OF MODERN FRENCH

Along with Italian, Spanish, Portuguese, and Romanian, French belongs to the family of Romance languages. These evolved from the Latin tongue used by the Roman conquerors. The people in the ancient region of modern France spoke a Celtic language known as Gaulish when the Romans conquered them. About 350 words in modern French can be traced to Gaulish.

The Frankish invasion contributed about 1,000 words to modern French, along with the name of the country. Danish Vikings added roughly 90 words. During the Renaissance, many words came into the language from Latin and Greek. Neighbors Italy and Spain also contributed many words to French.

Old French was spoken from the ninth to the 14th century. It had two main dialects: *langue d'oc* ("LAHNG DOHK") in the south and *langue d'oïl* ("LAHNG DOYL") in the north. *Oc* and *oïl* were the words used to mean "yes." The northern Francien dialect became the standard French language of the country, because Paris was so influential. The dialect of the south survives in the regional dialect called Provençal.

Charlemagne distinguished between the "rustic Romance tongue" and the "Latin tongue" and proposed the use of the former in church services. The first known written document in French was the Oaths of Strasbourg, a treaty signed in A.D. 842. It was not until the 16th century that French totally replaced Latin as the language for official documents.

Regional dialects are still spoken, especially at the edges of the country. They include Alsatian, Basque, Breton, Catalan, Flemish, and Provençal. As some dialects have diminished in importance, French scholars have grown increasingly interested in studying and preserving them.

Regional dialects, some older than the French language, are still spoken in various parts of the country.

THE ACADÉMIE FRANÇAISE

"It is a tradition solidly established in France to see in the purity of the language the image of the grandeur of the state."

—linguist Claude Hagège

The official guardian of the purity and glory of French language and literature is the Académie Française, or French Academy. Originally an informal coterie of literary men who met in Paris in the early 1630s to discuss rhetoric and criticism, the Academy was founded in 1635 by Cardinal de Richelieu. His goal was to make French a universal language, like Latin, and to make it clear and stable. He succeeded so well that the French language earned particular praise for the clear meaning of words and logical rules of grammar. These virtues are also assets in conducting international business and diplomacy.

There are 40 Academy members, known as the "40 Immortals." They are chosen from among France's leading writers, scientists, politicians, military leaders, lawyers, and church leaders. The first woman member, Belgian-born author and U.S.-French citizen Marguerite Yourcenar, was elected in 1980; and the first Asian member, Chinese writer, poet, and translator François Cheng, was elected in 2002.

Members meet weekly, and they serve for life. They are initiated wearing ceremonial swords, cocked hats, and elaborate uniforms embroidered with green palms.

The Academy's main task is to write and edit *The Dictionary of the French Academy* (*Le Dictionnaire de l'Académie française*), the ultimate authority on the French language. The Academy's work has discouraged rapid changes in the language, enabling modern readers to understand easily French literature written many centuries ago. Some have accused the Academy of being too conservative. However, after World War II, more than 2,000 English words entered the French language—words like *le weekend, le drugstore*, and *le hamburger*. The awarding of literary prizes has also been an important function of the French Academy.

BODY LANGUAGE

You can tell whether people are French just by watching them talk. The French use their entire faces to emphasize what they are saying: raised eyebrows, wrinkled foreheads, broad smiles. Lips purse to form the vowel sounds. The

hands are always moving, especially among people in the south.

French body language is fairly easy to understand. The shoulder shrug means "I don't know," "I don't care," or "There's nothing I can do about it." Two outstretched hands, palms up and fingers spread, can mean helplessness, anger, or indifference. A circle made of thumb and forefinger with the other three fingers raised means "OK" or, better yet, "perfect."

KEEPING THE LANGUAGE PURE

Both the French educational system and the conservative French Academy help to standardize the usage and pronunciation of French words throughout the country. Thus, people from all parts of France and of every social class can easily understand one another.

In the 1970s the French government outlawed the use of any foreign word in official documents, on radio and television, and in advertising, if an equivalent French word already existed. Officially, the French view English words cropping up in their language as an invasion that is sure to have disastrous consequences.

Unofficially, younger and more casual French people like the flexibility of English words and phrases. As writer Carl Bernstein observed, it is easy to combine words into catchy new expressions in English but almost impossible in French.

In matters of language, France has exported at least as much as it has imported. English has borrowed words from French since the Norman Conquest of England in 1066. It is estimated that 40 to 45 percent of all English words have French origins. Borrowed words reflect everything from religion—*pray, penance*, and *faith*—to French leadership in fashion and food—*chic, gourmet*, and *vogue*. French synonyms are generally more abstract and intellectual, and English synonyms more human and concrete. The French language has also lent countless words to languages in Europe, Asia, and Africa.

In 1991 the government decreed many radical spelling changes involving plural forms, hyphens (*le blue-jean* became *le bluejean*), and accent marks. The French Academy at first approved the changes, but later the members changed their minds and rejected the reforms. Many French writers organized to resist the changes, but there is a precedent for such rules imposed from on high. In 1740 the French Academy itself decreed spelling changes for one-quarter of the words then in use.

ENGLISH WITH A FRENCH TWIST

The English language has been enriched by many French words and expressions, such as *attaché, billet-doux, bon voyage, café, carte blanche, chalet, chef, civilisation, crème de la crème, de rigueur, fait accompli, faux pas, genre, glacial, réndez-vous*, RSVP (*répondez s'il vous plait*), *restaurant, valet*, and *vis-à-vis*.

The English word "billiards" comes from the French word *billard*, "employee" from *employé*, "employer" from *l'employeur*, "journalist" from *journaliste*, "merit" from *mériter*, "nonsense" from *non-sens*, "occasion" from *occasionner*, "platform" from *plate-forme*, "rabble" from *râble*, and "telegraph" from *télégraphe*.

A war on words has started between France and Britain. Concerned about the proliferation of English in the French language, the French government is actively promoting a ban on the public display of some 3,000 English terms in France. The English have threatened to counter any ban on their language in France by abolishing French words from their own language.

Magazine publishing is a flourishing industry in France. There are magazines for all kinds of tastes and interests.

THE PRESS

Freedom of the French press is guaranteed by the Declaration of the Rights of Man. Since 1939 the number of daily newspapers published in France has shrunk from 220 to 92. Of these 13 come from Paris.

In 2002 two free dailies, *Metro* and *20 Minutes*, began circulating in the public transportation systems in Paris, Lyon, and Marseille. These new papers strongly challenge leading ones like the liberal *Le Monde* ("Luh Mohnd"), or *The World*; the conservative *Le Figaro* ("Luh Fee-gah-ROH"); and the sports daily *L'Equipe* ("L'ay-KEEP"), or *The Team*.

Publishing has spread to the provinces. The avid French reader can pore over international, national, regional, and local news and get a wide range of political opinions. The regional paper with the widest circulation is *Ouest-France*, or *West-France*, published in Brittany's capital of Rennes.

Magazine publishing has mushroomed, with the emergence of special-interest magazines covering the youth market, sports, women's concerns, business, the media, religion, home improvement, health, the arts and sciences, and of course the news. *Paris Match* is photojournalistic and is the most popular magazine in the news category. More popular still are the entertainment weeklies *Télé 7 Jours* ("Tay-lay set ZHOOR"), or *TV 7 Days*, and *Télé Z* ("Tay-lay Zed"), each with more than 2.4 million readers.

Of the French-based international news agencies, the largest is *L'Agence France-Presse* (AFP), founded in 1944 and operating in about 165 countries around the world, of which 110 have AFP bureaus and 50 are covered by local correspondents.

RADIO AND TELEVISION

The French government administers Radio France's five local stations and Radio France International's numerous stations, reaching an estimated potential audience of 80 million listeners worldwide. In addition, some 1,800 private, local radio stations broadcast round-the-clock programs over FM frequencies. Near the borders, French audiences can pick up both radio and television broadcasts from neighboring Luxembourg and Monte Carlo, and other foreign countries.

Almost every French home has at least one radio, 95 percent of French households have

Christophe Dechavanne is one of the most famous television entertainers in the country. A number of French radio and television personalities have attained star status.

television, 65 percent have VCRs, and DVD is catching on. There are three public television channels, one of them hosting the programs of the Franco-German joint venture the *Association Relative à la Télévision Européenne* (ARTE), plus 130 different channels, general, regional, or thematic. The most viewed are private open channels *TF1* and *M6*, and pay-TV channel Canal Plus, with over a million exclusive subscribers.

Nine percent of the French have cable, 1 million households are equipped for satellite television, and 16 million people subscribe to pay-TV. France is getting prepared for a new system, *Télévision Numérique Terrestre* (TNT), or Terrestrial Numerical Television, to replace hertz frequencies with ground transmission. About half of all programs shown on French television are imported from other countries, especially the United States. The government continues to uphold the educational and cultural level of French television and to resist American influences.

ARTS

THE ARTS HAVE FLOURISHED IN FRANCE for thousands of years. Prehistoric drawings some 17,000 years old adorn the walls of the famous caves of Lascaux in southwestern France. France is adorned with many styles of architecture, with ancient buildings often standing alongside controversial modern constructions.

THE GLORIES OF FRENCH ARCHITECTURE

Decorated prehistoric caves and Celtic graves containing jewelry and helmets are evidence of the earliest settlers. Roman civilization left marvels of construction—aqueducts, amphitheaters, and scattered ruins— throughout the country. In the Middle Ages, Romanesque churches, abbeys, and castles were built in a heavy and solid style, with round arches and flattened columns.

The Gothic style, from the mid-12th through the 15th centuries, makes use of pointed arches, ribbed ceiling vaults, colorful stained-glass windows, delicate spires reaching to the heavens, and elaborate decoration with religious statues. Notre-Dame Cathedral in Paris, built from 1163 to 1350, is famous for its daring, single-arched flying buttresses and its three 13th-century rose windows. The medieval abbey of Mont-Saint-Michel, off the coast of Normandy, has aspects of both Romanesque and Gothic styles.

Renaissance architecture from the 16th and 17th centuries revived classical forms such as the Roman arch, the dome, and Corinthian columns. Renaissance buildings, such as the chateau built for Francis I at Chambord, are harmonious and symmetrical.

THE EIFFEL TOWER

A symbol of Paris since it was built for France's Centennial Exposition of 1889, the striking 984-foot (300-m) Eiffel Tower was the tallest building in the world until 1930. Its construction of open-lattice wrought iron was a technological breakthrough, designed by bridge engineer Gustave Eiffel.

The revolutionary height and arresting design provoked great controversy 100 years ago. The tower was almost demolished in 1909 but was saved to house transmitters for the first transatlantic wireless telephones. Today, the Eiffel Tower holds radio and television transmitters, three restaurants, a post office, and a steady stream of visitors who ride to the top for a dazzling view over Paris.

The baroque period that followed saw an interest in the dramatic, luxurious, and sensual. Buildings combined architecture, painting, and sculpture and were integrated with elaborate gardens, lakes, fountains, clipped trees, hedges, and flowerbeds laid out in formal patterns, such as in the Tuileries and at Versailles. François Mansart's church of Val-de-Grâce in Paris is an excellent example of French baroque—rich yet subtle.

Succeeding styles—rococo (or late baroque), neoclassical, art nouveau, art deco, modern, and postmodern—reflected the changing lifestyles of the French people and the new technologies available to builders. Emphasis shifted from buildings for the Church, kings, and nobles to structures for the public.

Baron Haussman's 19th-century urban plans enhanced Paris's beauty. Skyscrapers, where possible, were placed far from the center, with space reserved for parks. The Parisian sidewalks and wide, straight tree-lined avenues were also his work. Different regions in France have their own distinctive architectural details, each town having its own unique charm.

The Louvre Museum in Paris has been under construction, on and off, since the 16th century and provides a unique showcase for the history of French architecture. In 1989 a controversial new entrance was built—a 71-foot-high (22-m-high) steel and glass pyramid, designed by American architect I. M. Pei. The Louvre's painting collection is one of the largest in the world, representing all periods of European art up to the Impressionists.

CHATEAUS AND PALACES

Chateaus, combinations of the medieval feudal castle and the Italian villa, are among the most beautiful examples of French Renaissance and Gothic architecture. A string of beautiful chateaus stretches along the valley of the Loire River. Some of the finest are at Blois, Chambord, Amboise, Chaumont, and Chenonceaux. Most were built and redesigned over several centuries.

France's chateaus were often the stage of religious conflicts and quarrels over successions to the throne that sometimes led to murder and revenge. Many are still filled with elegant antique furnishings, paintings, and tapestries and are surrounded by gorgeous gardens. The chateau built for Francis I at Chambord has 440 rooms, 365 fireplaces, 13 great staircases, stables to hold 1,200 horses, and stands in a park surrounded by a wall 22 miles (35.4 km) in circumference.

The chateau of Chenonceaux, which bridges the Cher River, was confiscated by François I. Later, Henri II presented it to his favorite mistress, Diane de Poitiers. When Henri II died, his queen, Catherine de Médicis, forced de Poitiers to exchange it for Chaumont-sur-Loire. The chateau of Ussé looks like a fairytale castle and is said to have inspired the story of *Sleeping Beauty*.

Near Paris, the spectacular palaces of Versailles and Fontainebleau functioned as hunting lodges and homes for royalty and their retinue of thousands of nobles, servants, artists, and soldiers. At Fontainebleau, Louis XIV revoked the Edict of Nantes, France and Rome signed the Concordat, and Napoleon Bonaparte signed his abdication. The many important historical events that occurred at Versailles span the beginnings of the French Revolution to the signing, in its Hall of Mirrors, of the Treaty of Versailles by the Allies and Germany in 1919.

VISUAL ARTS THAT ILLUMINATE OUR WORLD

The first paintings in France were the work of Cro-Magnon cave dwellers. They drew wild animals—reindeer, horses, and bisons—on the walls of their caves, perhaps hoping for magical assistance in the hunt.

Manuscript illumination flourished in the Middle Ages, but a French school of painting emerged only in the 17th century. Leading baroque artists included Georges de La Tour and the Le Nain brothers. Claude Lorrain and Nicolas Poussin were masters of ideal landscape painting. Charles Le Brun was court painter to Louis XIV.

In the 18th century, rococo painters Jean-Antoine Watteau, François Boucher, and Jean-Honoré Fragonard were leading court artists who celebrated the theater and beauty and romance, while Jean-Baptiste-Siméon Chardin became known for simpler domestic scenes and still lifes. Elisabeth Vigée-Lebrun became popular as Marie Antoinette's portrait painter. Jacques-Louis David, court painter to Louis XVI, was the prime illustrator of the Revolution and the Napoleonic era. Romantic painter Eugène Delacroix's *The 28th July: Liberty Leading the People* was inspired by the French Revolution. Honoré Daumier satirized the professional classes. Also famous are the Classicist painter Jean-Baptiste-Camille Corot and Realists Jean-François Millet and Gustave Courbet.

Many important art movements began in Paris, even though many notable artists were of foreign birth, such as Marc Chagall, Salvador Dalí, Leonor Fini, Alberto Giacometti, Vincent Van Gogh, Amadeo Modigliani, Pablo Picasso, and Victor Vasarely.

Visual arts that illuminate our world

Anyone who wishes to become familiar with French painting could do worse than to study the works of Edgar Degas, Edouard Manet, Pierre-Auguste Renoir, Claude Monet, Paul Gauguin, Henri Matisse, Henri Rousseau, Georges Braque, Paul Cézanne, or Henri de Toulouse-Lautrec. They have left vivid images of the people, landscape, food, and flowers of France.

Revolutionary art movements in France developed in stunning succession: Impressionism, Expressionism, Symbolism, Fauvism, Cubism, Dada, and Surrealism. Through their handling of line and color, painters expressed their personal emotions, dreams, and subconscious impulses or their cooler intellectual concerns. Twentieth-century local and foreign-born painters Balthus, Alberto Giacometti, Sonia Delaunay, Jean Dubuffet, Leonor Fini, Yves Klein, Victor Vasarely, and others turned out innovative masterpieces that have enriched museum collections around the world. But it is perhaps Matisse who is best remembered as one of the greatest French artists of the 20th century for his long, creative lifespan during which he produced a stunning array of works in varied styles.

French painters also applied their talents to sculpture, ceramics, collage, weaving and tapestry, and other decorative arts. Museums proudly display the sculpture of Degas, Dubuffet, Aristide Maillol, Jean Arp, Matisse, and many others. Probably France's foremost sculptor was Auguste Rodin (1840–1917), famous for the works *The Thinker* and *The Kiss*. Most major museums own copies of Rodin's work and there are museums in Paris, Philadelphia, and Tokyo dedicated to him.

The visual arts reach the public in many guises. American writer Richard Bernstein singled out the comic strip as the most popular cultural form in France. Called the *bande dessinée* ("BAHND deh-see-NAY"), or B.D. for short, this art form enjoys a large and devoted following. Famous examples include *The Adventures of Tintin* and *Astérix*.

The Marsupilami is a fantastic animal whose adventures are told in B.D. form.

FRENCH IMPRESSIONISM

French Impressionism is so widely loved today that it is hard to imagine the fury it provoked when its artists first showed their work in Paris. The appearance of Edouard Manet's *Luncheon on the Grass* in an 1863 exhibition touched off the revolutionary new art movement.

It was Claude Monet who gave the movement its name, from his 1872 *An Impression, Sunrise.* The Impressionists organized eight of their own exhibitions in the 1870s and 1880s. The core artists were Monet, Sisley, Pissarro, and Renoir. Although their interests and styles differed, they cooperated in exhibiting their work and greatly influenced one another.

The Impressionists stressed color and composition over story content, emotions, and symbols, and sought to capture the transient effects of light and color. They worked outdoors, used small canvases, and made freer brushstrokes to capture the quickly changing atmosphere. Collectors delight in the Impressionist images of light and color, sunny landscapes and shimmering water.

Among the most fascinating Impressionist paintings are Monet's series of pictures of poplar trees, haystacks, water lilies, and the Rouen Cathedral. He painted the same scenes at different times of the day, trying to capture the fleeting effects of light on the ever-changing natural world. Renoir was known for sensuous, colorful pictures of pretty women and children and joyous crowd scenes. Degas portrayed bathers and dancers.

An assortment of styles and subjects characterized the many great Post-Impressionist artists who followed: Toulouse-Lautrec's Moulin Rouge cabaret dancers, Cézanne's landscapes that so greatly influenced Cubism, Gauguin's exotic scenes of Tahiti and the South Pacific, and Dutch painter Van Gogh's colorful, often tortured still lifes and portraits. Van Gogh and Gauguin moved beyond Impressionism to use color for its emotional, expressive, and decorative elements.

After a long struggle for recognition, Impressionist and Post-Impressionist paintings received international critical approval and now sell for very high prices.

LITERATURE OF IDEAS AND PASSION

French writers and thinkers have had a lasting impact on French politics, their ideas the seeds for riots, revolution, and reform. For example, philosopher Jean-Jacques Rousseau's *The Social Contract* is said to have inspired the French Revolution.

Of the poetry and love songs of medieval France, the best known are *The Romance of the Rose* and the earlier *The Song of Roland*, a mid-11th-century epic based on a minor battle during Charlemagne's Spanish campaigns. France produced one of Europe's first professional woman writers, Christine de Pisan, born in 1364, who wrote numerous poems of courtly love, a biography of Charles V of France, and several works in defence of women. Marguerite de Navarre's remarkable *Heptameron*, published posthumously in 1558 and modeled on Boccaccio's *Decameron*, contained short stories told by fictional characters, probably one of the earliest French tales written in prose. One French work still popular today is *Gargantua and Pantagruel* by Renaissance writer and humanist François Rabelais, whose style of coarse humor gave rise to the term "Rabelaisian." The classical age was a high point in French literature, especially during the reign of Louis XIV. In the 17th and 18th centuries, playwrights Pierre Corneille and Jean Racine wrote tragedies, while Jean-Baptiste Poquelin Molière wrote comedies poking fun at human frailty.

French was the language of the educated class all over Europe, and French arts and literature were widely admired. The mathematician and creator of analytic geometry René Descartes wrote the famous words "I think, therefore I am," thus inspiring modern philosophy.

Eighteenth-century Enlightenment writers included the brilliant and prolific Voltaire. He opposed tyranny and prejudice and wrote lampoons on the French Regency and the famous satire *Candide*. Denis Diderot and

"Man was born free, but he is everywhere in chains."

—*The opening lines of* The Social Contract.

One of the most famous women writers in France was George Sand, who wrote novels, short stories, and letters for adults and children.

Jean d'Alembert edited the *Encyclopédie,* an influential work of radical opinion. A Romantic reaction against the Age of Reason led to the glorification of emotion and imagination. Swiss-born Jean-Jacques Rousseau's *The Social Contract* argued that if a civil society could be based on a genuine social contract with individuals, men would obtain true political freedom. Poet, playwright, and novelist Victor Hugo was another leading Romantic writer. He wrote *The Hunchback of Notre Dame* and *Les Misérables*, the latter heavily influenced by the Revolution and an appeal for social justice.

Alexandre Dumas's adventures *The Three Musketeers* and *The Count of Monte Cristo* are still enjoyed today. Jules Verne's novels were the forerunners of modern science fiction. An enduring favorite is Antoine de Saint-Exupéry's enchanting fable, *The Little Prince.*

Gustave Flaubert wrote his famous *Madame Bovary* in a realistic style. Émile Zola carried realism even further in a style called naturalism, exploring the squalid lives of the poor. The erudite man of letters, Anatole France, won the Nobel Prize for Literature in 1921.

In the early 1900s, Marcel Proust wrote his epic *Remembrance of Things Past*, which many people consider the greatest modern French novel. André Gide won the Nobel Prize for literature in 1947 and raised ideas that led into the French Existentialism of the World War II period. Jean-Paul Sartre and Algerian-born Albert Camus developed these ideas of free will and moral responsibility in their novels and plays, and each won a Nobel Prize, although Sartre turned his down in 1964.

More recent writers of note include Alain Robbe-Grillet, Claude Simon, who won the Nobel Prize in 1985, Marguerite Duras, Nathalie Sarraute, Marguerite Yourcenar, and Michel Butor.

One of the best-loved French literary characters for children is Babar the Elephant, created by father and son Jean and Laurent de Brunhoff.

FRENCH MUSIC

French music continues to delight audiences around the world. Georges Bizet's opera *Carmen* and Maurice Ravel's *Boléro* are well-known from live performances and recordings but also as background music to Olympic skating competitions and Hollywood films.

Until the 19th century, France imported more music than it created. The few early French composers of note were François Couperin and Jean Philippe Rameau in the 18th century. As with the other arts, the French appreciate originality and experimentation in music. Hector Berlioz and Claude Debussy were 19th-century pioneers whose influence in music mirrored the revolutionary contributions of French painters of their time. Debussy's subtle tonal shadings and the sense of painting a picture with sound have led critics to call it Impressionist. A leading 20th-century innovator, composer-conductor Pierre Boulez created music in the 12-tone scale and also blended tape recordings with live music in a form called "concrete music." Olivier Messiaen introduced into Western music unfamiliar modes from the Middle Ages, music from Japan, rhythms from India, and sounds from nature, especially the songs of birds, and tried to express his Roman Catholic faith through music.

Municipal opera houses are found in many of the large cities, including the famous Paris Opera House. In Paris, classical music is performed at the Conservatoire and the Salle des Concerts. Salle Pleyel is home to the *Orchestre de Paris*, and the Théâtre Musical de Paris houses the *Orchestre National de France*. Concerts are also regularly performed at the Théâtre des Champs-Elysées. Regional music festivals flourish, especially in the south. All forms of music, from chamber to jazz, have their stars and their enthusiastic fans. More than 25,000 local rock groups attract tremendous support, especially from teenagers.

"There is no theory. You have only to listen. Pleasure is the law. I love music passionately. And because I love it, I try to free it from barren traditions that stifle it. It is a free art gushing forth, an open-air art boundless as the elements, the wind, the sky, the sea. It must never be shut in and become an academic art."

—*Claude Debussy*

The Moulin Rouge is most famous for its French cancan shows and cabaret revues.

MINUET, CANCAN, AND BALLET

The minuet was a popular court dance from the 17th century for about 150 years, performed at first with small, graceful steps, then later with grand elegance. Ballet came to France from Italy and flourished from the 16th century. Its popularity waned but was revived in Paris around 1909 by the dazzling performances of the Ballets Russes, headed by Sergey Diaghilev. Popular 19th-century French ballets include *La Sylphide* and *Giselle*. French dancer and choreographer Marius Petipa created the immensely popular *Sleeping Beauty* and *The Nutcracker*.

Known for its high kicks revealing the petticoats and legs of the women dancers, the cancan became popular in Parisian dance halls in the 1830s. In the 19th century, Jacques Offenbach created a French comic opera called the *opérette*, and his *Gaîté Parisienne* is still popular today.

African-American dancer and singer Josephine Baker became famous in Paris in the 1920s for her spirited, semi-nude dancing and for her habit of strolling the Champs-Elysées with a diamond-collared pet leopard.

Today, many ballet companies thrive in Paris and the provinces. Known internationally are the Lyon Opera Ballet and the prestigious Paris Opera Ballet School.

FILMS

The French were major pioneers in filmmaking in the 1890s. The first motion picture was invented in 1895 by the French brothers Auguste and Louis Lumière. Some outstanding earlier directors were Marcel Pagnol, Marcel Carné, René Clair, Jean Renoir, and Jean Cocteau. Classic French films from the 1950s include the original *Cyrano de Bergerac* by José Ferrer, Roger Vadim's *And God Created Woman* (starring Brigitte Bardot), and Alain Resnais's *Hiroshima Mon Amour* (*Hiroshima My Love*).

One of many movie theaters in Paris advertises its shows.

Some important directors of the French New Wave (1958–64) were François Truffaut, Jean-Luc Godard, Claude Chabrol, Jacques Rivette, and Eric Rohmer. Focusing on film technique rather than plot, they often improvised their scripts. In the 1980s and 1990s, directors such as Luc Besson (*The Fifth Element, The Big Blue*) and Jean-Jacques Annaud (*The Name of the Rose*) turned to more elaborate sets and costumes. A landmark French film in 2001 was Jean-Pierre Jeunet's *Le fabuleux destín d'Amélie Poulain* (*Amélie From Montmartre*).

French films have been perceived by the rest of the world as sensual, poignant, political, literary, and highly personal visions of the human condition. The French produce about 150 full-length feature films each year. The annual international film festival at Cannes is the most prestigious in the industry.

LEISURE

IN EARLIER TIMES, the typical French farmer finished a long day of vigorous activity in the fields and spent any free hours quietly. The favorite pastime was arguing politics and relaxing by reading the paper or perhaps dozing under it.

Today, French people enjoy a shorter official work week of 35 hours, with five weeks of vacation. Families enjoy gardening, working on home improvement, reading, and watching television. Increasingly, they spend their leisure time plunging into active sports in the pursuit of physical fitness and "the good life."

More French schools are adding sports programs. Schools and communities are building more gyms, swimming pools, and playing fields. The sports-minded French have led in world-class sports competitions, winning many top honors in the 2002 Olympic Games.

Left: **Many people go on vacation twice a year, in the summer and in the winter. Winter vacations are usually spent skiing in the Alps.**

Opposite: **Mountain climbing is a favorite leisure activity.**

TEAM AND INDIVIDUAL SPORTS

The French play and watch soccer, which they call football, in huge numbers. Each region has its own team, and there are nearly 8,000 soccer clubs. They also play basketball, volleyball, and rugby football. Both men and women compete in boxing, judo, and other individual contests.

The French can be quite serious about their sports, even wildly competitive. Cockfights in the north and bullfights in the south roused fierce passions in earlier times.

More popular than team sports are individual pursuits. The French ride horses and bicycles, jog, ice skate, camp, and hike. They climb mountains, and once up may choose to descend by hang-gliding.

The French head to the water to swim, sail, canoe, windsurf, and water ski. They also ski on snow over vast expanses of mountainous terrain. The 1992 Winter Olympic Games were hosted by Albertville in the Alps. Tennis is no longer a sport for the rich only, as each year more public courts are being built. Golf is still fairly exclusive, played on private courses in large cities and resort areas.

Spectator sports like horse races remain popular. Three famous auto races are the Le Mans 24-hour race, the Monte Carlo Rally, and the Grand Prix. Tennis championships, including the French Open (one of the international Grand Slam tournaments), and the Bol d'Or motorcycle race at Le Mans draw enthusiastic fans. The Tour de France, a 20-day bicycle race across the country, is France's most popular spectator sport.

The French love the beach, not just to swim and sunbathe, but also to practice other sports.

TOUR DE FRANCE

Most daily activities all over France come to a halt during the annual Tour de France bicycle race. Millions watch it on television or go out to join the cheering crowds lining the 2,500-mile (4,022-km) route. Each July, close to 200 professional racers from many countries compete in this event, although around 40 drop out before the end. Each racer must belong to a team of nine riders, with varying special skills in climbing or sprinting.

This race, held for the first time in 1903, winds through many regions of France, including extremely steep mountain roads. Those who finish ride proudly down the Champs-Elysées through the Arc de Triomphe in Paris. The cyclist with the best time at the end of each day wears the coveted yellow vest on the following day as he struggles to retain his lead. Most overall winners have been French, but American Lance Armstrong has won four competitions in a row from 1999 to 2002.

The Tour de France means big business. Large sums are won and lost by gamblers on the race. The winning cyclist becomes a millionaire through endorsements and advertising, and manufacturers of cars, bicycles, sports clothes, and soft drinks compete to have their products appear on television being used by the heroes of the day.

The Tour de France is open only to men. The shorter Tour de France Féminin was set up for women racers in 1984.

Guignol was a popular 18th-century puppet character. Today the name is used to refer to the puppet show.

OTHER LEISURE PURSUITS

French people pursue every kind of hobby, from photography to ceramics, from collecting antiques to playing musical instruments, from bird watching to stamp collecting. Like the farmers of old, the French still hunt and fish, and both freshwater and deep-sea fishing are popular leisure pursuits.

The French also read and watch television and attend cultural events in their leisure time. They enjoy Scrabble, crossword puzzles, card games, chess, and bridge.

They follow Voltaire's advice to cultivate their gardens, and they spend significant amounts of time and money on improvements to their home, including their vacation homes.

In the big cities, there are lots of things to do for leisure. Especially in Paris, families visit the many large and small museums, the aquarium, the planetarium, and the wax museum. Leisure in the parks is especially delightful for children, who enjoy puppet shows, donkey rides, sailing rented miniature boats on ponds, visiting zoos, and riding on carousels and miniature trains.

The French version of the Punch and Judy puppet shows, known as *Théâtre Guignol* ("teh-AH-truh guee-NYOHL"), originated in the region of Lyonnais in the 19th century. Guignol, a hand puppet dressed in regional garb, with a short nose and round eyes, is always surprised and easily cheated but quick to get himself out of trouble and to help his friends. These shows demand active audience participation and teach the young audience about French culture and dialogue.

Entire families flock to Parc Astérix north of Paris every day. This theme park was inspired by the popular French cartoon strip about characters from ancient Gaul who resisted the Roman invasion of France 2,000 years ago.

The European Disneyland in Marne-la-Vallée brings an international flavor to France's leisure scene. This $4.4 billion project covers more than 7.8 square miles (20.2 square km) of former sugar beet fields 20 miles (32 km) east of Paris. The whole park covers an area one-fifth the size of Paris. Both the *Métro* and the TGV bring visitors speedily to the theme park, where they can find accommodation in one of seven hotels.

Astérix is a cartoon character created by Goscinny and Uderzo a few decades ago. Modern readers of the comic strip can now mingle with the Gallic heroes at the Parc Astérix.

While it features Mickey Mouse and all the other popular American attractions, Disneyland Paris has a more European flavor. For example, the new Discoveryland is based on the science fiction of French novelist Jules Verne, and Snow White speaks German.

Frequent protests and demonstrations by farmers, former residents, and ultra-rightists have somewhat marred the success of Disneyland Paris, which experienced considerable losses during its first years of operation. Its opponents view it as an American product transplanted into the French countryside and thus a threat to their culture.

The Aqualud water leisure center at Le Touquet beach. In the summer months, the beaches of France are crowded with vacationers.

VACATIONS

In the summer, nearly half the French population heads for the beach, most often between July 14 and August 31, clogging the nation's highways. One-quarter of the French population vacation abroad, with Spain, Italy, and Greece among the more popular destinations.

A great interest in health also spills over into the choice of leisure activities. On the highways, rest stops have been set up to include running tracks, obstacle courses, and exercise equipment. Some vacation centers combine sports with such health treatments as seawater therapy and mudbaths. Center Parcs, a popular vacation village near Paris, features a swimming pool with wave machines and water slides.

The French, like foreign tourists, sometimes take hot-air balloon rides through the wine country of the Loire Valley and Burgundy. They admire the countryside from barges that cruise the inland waterways. Other vacation activities include boating, painting, or retiring to a villa in the countryside.

BOULES, PÉTANQUE, AND PELOTE

French men particularly enjoy *boules*, a form of bowling without the pins. Each player throws two large metal balls in turn at a smaller ball. The small target ball is called *cochonnet* ("koh-shuh-NAY"), or piglet, and the object is to land your ball closest to it. The rules allow for knocking the other players' balls away, and onlookers are generous with advice to the players.

Pétanque ("peh-TAHNK") is a similar bowling game played with metal balls that are thrown into the air rather than rolled along the ground. It is particularly popular in the south, where groups gather in the village square for a casual game.

In the southwest, people play the Basque game of *pelote* ("peh-LOHT"). The players may wear gloves to hit the ball against a wall.

Vacation camps are also popular. In fact, the ultimate leisure camp comes from France—Club Med, which operates about 120 resorts called "villages" in some 40 countries and attracts people from all over the world. Each Club Med destination offers equipment and lessons for a variety of sports, especially water sports. Visitors can also enjoy sightseeing tours to sites such as the Mayan ruins near Cancún in Mexico, courses to improve computer skills, and language and art classes.

FESTIVALS

WHEN FRENCH CHILDREN GROW UP to write books or make movies about their lives, some of the happiest moments they recall are of celebrating festivals with their families. Some of their celebrations are widely known outside of France: Christmas, Easter, and New Year's festivities. Others, such as the Bastille Day celebration, are uniquely French. In either case, the French observe these occasions with tremendous energy and style. And, naturally, every French celebration includes wonderful things to eat and drink.

PUBLIC HOLIDAYS

There are 11 public holidays in France representing religious, national, and historic reasons for celebration. The six religious holidays reflect France's Roman Catholic history. These include *Pâques* ("PAH-kuh"), or Easter (a Monday in March or April), Ascension Day (a Thursday in May), Pentecost (the 49th day or seventh Sunday after Easter), the Feast of the Assumption (August 15), *Toussaint* ("too-SAN"), or All Saints' Day (November 1), and *Noël* ("noh-EL"), or Christmas (December 25).

HOLIDAYS FOR THE FAMILY

A holiday especially for children is the Epiphany, celebrated on January 6, coinciding with Twelfth Night, 12 nights after Christmas. A large round pastry called *la galette des rois* ("lah gah-LEHT day RWAH"), the cake of kings, containing a single bean is served. The youngest child present cuts the cake and passes out the pieces. Whoever finds the bean becomes the king or queen for the holiday and chooses a royal mate.

Candlemas, on February 2, is a religious holiday involving a Mass with candles carried in a procession. Families cook thin pancakes called *crêpes* ("KREPP"), and everyone tries flipping them. Legend has it that flipping the *crêpes* while holding a coin will bring happiness and wealth.

Parades and fireworks are the order of the day on Bastille Day.

Civil holidays include New Year's Day on January 1, Labor Day on May 1, and three additional dates that mark historical events.

Bastille Day, July 14, commemorates the storming of the Bastille prison in 1789, an event that sparked off the French Revolution. Also known as *Le Quatorze Juillet* ("luh kah-TORZ zhwee-YAY"), or July 14, this day is also France's national holiday. Tricolor flags appear on monuments and buses. Brass bands and military parades fill the streets. In Paris, military troops parade past the French president, and people crowd around the monument to the Bastille, where there are bands and dances. After dark the skies blaze with fireworks, and crowds of people dance in the streets.

A particularly spirited observance of this holiday in the medieval walled town of Carcassonne in the south is accompanied by spectacular fireworks and a festival of music, theater, and dance that lasts for two weeks.

Armistice Day, November 11, commemorates the end of World War I in 1918. Victory Day, May 8, celebrates the end of World War II in 1945. This holiday is sometimes called the Day of Liberty and Peace.

HOLIDAY REVELRY

Celebrations around Christmas and New Year's Day are particularly joyous. On Christmas Eve, French families gather to feast on turkey and, for dessert, a traditional Yule log, the *bûche de Noël* ("byesh duh Noh-EL"). Old and young share gifts, as in Christian countries around the world.

Sometimes children put out their shoes at bedtime for Père Noël ("PEHR Noh-EL"), or Father Christmas, to fill with gifts during the night. Naughty children get a whip instead of toys, delivered by Père Fouettard ("PEHR Foo-eh-TAHR"), or Father Spanker.

It was in the province of Alsace that Christmas trees first appeared in 1605. By the 19th century, they had become popular all over Europe and in the United States. In the mountains at Christmas skiers light up the night by descending the slopes with flaming torches.

New Year's Eve is celebrated with a feast and the honking of car horns at midnight. The following day people wish one another a Happy New Year and exchange gifts meant to bring good luck.

Carnival, or Mardi Gras, is celebrated in many French cities on Shrove Tuesday, the last day before the Roman Catholic observance of Lent. The observance of Carnival in Nice, on the French Riviera, began sometime in the 13th century. Today, partying goes on for weeks, with evening torch-light processions, parades of flower-covered floats, and huge groups of papier-mâché "big heads." Masked balls, confetti battles, flower tossing, and fireworks lead up to the moment when a model of King Carnival is set on fire, hanged, or drowned.

The carnival atmosphere of Mardi Gras as young people dress up in fancy costumes and party all night long.

115

Right: **For Christians, Easter is a time of rejoicing. Everyone goes to church, and children are given Easter eggs.**

April 1 is celebrated as *Poisson d'Avril* ("pwah-SAWN dahv-REEL"), or April Fish. This is something like April Fool's Day in the United States. In France, people try to pin a paper fish on someone's back without being caught. They laugh and point to the victim calling, *"Poisson d'avril!"* The person who is fooled is supposed to give the pranksters a chocolate fish in return.

Legend traces this holiday back to 1564, when Charles IX switched the beginning of the year from April 1 back to January 1. People protested mildly by exchanging silly gifts and playing pranks. Since the sun at

the time was in Pisces (the zodiac sign featuring two fish), candy fish as well as paper fish became associated with the holiday.

On Easter Monday, French children receive colored candy eggs and chocolate chickens. They may go to church in their best outfits and later hunt for Easter eggs. In France and Germany, handball playing is a traditional Easter amusement. The ball perhaps represents the sun, which is believed to take three leaps in rising on Easter morning.

On Labor Day, people exchange lilies of the valley and wear a blossom for good luck.

REGIONAL FESTIVALS AND SEASONAL EVENTS

Many areas of France have colorful festivals throughout the year. In Brittany, Quimper's Festival de Cornouaille, held every year since 1923, recalls the pre-Christian civilization of that region. Puppets act out Celtic tales, women demonstrate their embroidery skills, young girls model traditional lace headdresses, men engage in Breton wrestling matches, and people feast on grilled sardines and Breton *crêpes* while listening to bagpipe music and watching clog-stomping dancers.

A traditional festival in Burgundy features a jousting contest on the Yonne River. Two men carrying poles and shields stand in longboats. As the boats are rowed toward one another at full speed, each contestant tries to push the other into the water. This jousting is said to show off the skills of loggers who used to ride logs floated downriver to Paris.

In Brittany, men, women, and children wear charming traditional dress during local festivals.

In Alsace, a medieval festival at Ribeauvillé features knights in armor jousting, simulated bearbaiting, and parades of people grandly dressed as noble lords and ladies.

The Riviera city of Cannes welcomes some 40,000 film professionals to perhaps the most important film festival of the calendar year. The judges at Cannes review films from many countries, and their awards are reported in newspapers all over the world. Glamorous people-watching is an added attraction at this two-week festival.

Les Trois Glorieuses ("LAY TRWAH glaw-ree-YUHZ"), the Three Glorious Days, in November is France's chief wine festival, one of many fall harvest festivals. Three cities in Burgundy share the honors, and all are world-famous in wine-tasting circles: Beaune, Clos-de-Vougeot, and Meursault. On Sunday, a charity auction of wine is the highlight of the festival. On Monday, professionals and amateurs alike indulge in spirited wine tasting and folk dancing.

In Verdigny, the *Fête des Grappes Nouvelles* celebrates the end of the harvest. Wine tasters in ceremonial dress solemnly sample the wine.

Wine growers and drinkers also celebrate the appearance of the Beaujolais Nouveau, the new red wine in November. Grape harvest festivals, known as *Fête des Vendanges*, are widely celebrated in October. Members of old wine societies wear traditional clothes, and everyone tastes wine and dances. Even when it is not harvest time, the French can find a reason to rejoice. The wine villages pay tribute to their patron saint on St. Vincent's Day, January 22.

In addition to the grapevine, harvest festivals honor other gifts of the land, such as peaches in Roussillon, lavender in Digne, and apple cider in Normandy.

The long summer vacations enjoyed by French children and their families also coincide with festivals in many southern cities. Elaborate programs of concerts and plays, folk dancing, parades, and feasting attract French and foreign tourists.

France has nearly 500 summer music festivals, ranging from concerts on boats and in churches and historic chateaus to organ festivals in cathedrals with famous old organs and festivals devoted to folk, chamber, or jazz music.

Paris celebrates summer with music, dance, and drama during the Festival of the Marais, a city neighborhood, from mid-June to mid-July. Later in the summer, during the *Festival Estival de Paris* (Paris Summer Festival), Parisians enjoy classical concerts in churches, museums, and concert halls. The *Festival d'Automne à Paris* continues Paris's arts celebrations through the fall months, with colorful dance, theatre, and musical performances and art exhibitions.

Outside France but within easy celebrating distance are the festivals of Monaco, near Nice, such as the Monte-Carlo International Circus Festival in February, the Monte Carlo Motor Rally in January, the Monaco Grand Prix in May, and the International Fireworks Festival in midsummer.

Many festivals in France celebrate major events in the Roman Catholic Church. Most villages honor their patron saint with a festival.

LES SAINTES

An unusual gathering takes place near the end of May in the Mediterranean village of Saintes-Maries-de-la-Mer in the Camargue. Thousands of Gypsies come from all over Europe to honor their patron saint—Sarah of Egypt. They hold a candlelight vigil, then march in a procession from the church of Saintes-Maries to the sea, carrying holy statues of Saint Mary Salome and Saint Mary Jacobe. There, the statues are immersed in water, and little paper boats, each containing a flickering flame, are released into the sea. As part of the festivities, famous Gypsy entertainers strum guitars and perform for the dancing and clapping crowd.

In a region already known for colorful bullfights, flamingos, and wild horses, the Gypsies add the dramatic finishing touch. Another pilgrimage in October also attracts many pilgrims and thousands of onlookers.

FOOD

THE FRENCH PEOPLE care passionately about food. They invest a significant amount of time and money in the pursuit of fine meals. The French insist on fresh ingredients of high quality and shop carefully for the best value.

Great care is given to the production of both raw and processed food. Each person involved in farming, marketing, and processing is an important and respected link in the food industry. Generations of families devote themselves to producing exquisite fruit, vegetables, and cheeses. They develop special breeds of chickens, ducks, geese, cows, sheep, and hogs to better satisfy demanding French homemakers and restaurant patrons.

Above: **French cooks insist on the freshest fruit for their desserts.**

Opposite: **Different types of French bread in a sandwich shop.**

The French have written extensively about food for centuries, so that the cuisine is a rich field for study, with its own encyclopedias and histories full of original culinary genius and dynamic personalities. Rating restaurants is a national sport, and numerous guides on the subject are published each year.

The result is a cuisine that has a great influence on the food of other lands. International wine and food societies celebrate the recipes of France's greatest chefs.

Like people of other countries, some of the French are giving up their rich traditional dishes for lighter meals of salad and cold meats.

TYPES OF CUISINE

There are many types of meals to enjoy in France, depending on how much you can spend, where you are, and what you feel like eating. The most elaborate style of cooking, haute cuisine, describes the grand meal of multiple courses served by top restaurants.

The hearty meals cooked at home for a family are known as *cuisine bourgeoise*, which overlaps with *cuisine régionale* ("ray-zhuh-NAHL"), or regional cooking—dishes made from locally available ingredients served in the provinces.

In certain restaurants, the chef offers a set menu with many courses of fairly small portions, giving a sampler of the chef's specialties and the best foods of the season and the region.

Nouvelle ("noo-VELL") *cuisine* refers to a recent trend among French chefs to serve lighter food with little or no butter, cream, or flour in the sauces. Food is arranged artistically on the plate, which may be decorated with edible flowers. Meat and vegetables are only lightly cooked. The low-calorie dishes of *cuisine minceur* ("man-SIR") were introduced in the 1970s by a French chef in an attempt to fuse dieting and weight control with fine French cooking.

REGIONAL FOODS AND DISHES

Different regions of France are famous for special foods and cooking styles unique to that area. Regional recipes are often passed down from one generation to the next, preserved on family stoves and in the kitchens of inns and restaurants from province to province.

Oysters from Brittany are prized for their delicate flavor.

The highly prized ingredients and distinctive styles of regional cuisines can also be sampled in Paris, which, like any other cosmopolitan city, offers a wide variety of food. However, the prices of regional dishes are much higher in Paris than in the provinces. The French appreciate good regional cooking in the provinces where the ducks are fattened, the fish caught, or the truffles unearthed.

There is food of almost unlimited variety and thousands of ways to prepare it throughout France. Some French foods use ingredients that may be unfamiliar to foreigners: sea urchins, eel, snails, kidneys, calf's head, pig's trotters, little birds like woodcock and thrush, and all kinds of wild game.

In general, the cooking of northern France is based on butter, while southern French cooking uses olive oil, as does neighboring Italy. *Cuisine minceur* dishes use less butter and cream and more vegetable sauces.

One of the most famous regional foods of France, *pâté de foie gras* ("pah-TAY duh FWAH GRAH"), the famous liver spread made from specially, and sometimes cruelly, fattened ducks or geese, comes from the Périgord region in southwestern France and also from Alsace.

The waters of the English Channel and the Atlantic Ocean yield many varieties of mussels, oysters, and fish. From Provence come olives and herbs—bay leaf, fennel, rosemary, and thyme. Excellent pork dishes (hams, pâtés, terrines, and sausages—known collectively as *charcuterie*) differ from one region of France to another.

A famous white or pink chewy candy called nougat, filled with chopped almonds and cherries comes from the town of Montélimar. Dijon exports several styles of mustard. Privas, near Lyon, produces *marrons glacés* ("mah-ROHN glah-SAY"), a delicacy of candied chestnuts. The region of Burgundy is known for snails, Cavaillon for melons, and Normandy for butter, cream, cheese, and sparkling cider.

TRUFFLES: "BLACK DIAMONDS"

One of the most prized delicacies of French cuisine is the black truffle. This aromatic, black, warty fungus that looks like a deformed avocado, grows underground in the roots of oak and hazelnut trees. Trained dogs and pigs are adept at sniffing out these hidden treasures. Because they have not yet been successfully cultivated by farmers, truffles are rare. Scientists are trying to develop a machine to hunt them, claiming that pigs and dogs miss 80 percent of those in the ground.

Truffles are served whole or minced in sauces, eggs, and other dishes, providing a nutty flavor adored by the French. They are tastier fresh than canned, but are very expensive either way—a pound of the best truffles from the Périgord can easily cost thousands of dollars!

French food lovers and foreign tourists travel to Mont-Saint-Michel in Normandy to sample the famous local omelets. They seek the finest *bouillabaisse* ("boo-ya-BESS"), a fragrant fish stew, in Marseille. They head west to Toulouse to sample the perfect *cassoulet* ("kah-soo-LAY"), a complex casserole of white beans, lamb, pork, sausage, and poultry.

The origin of many a recipe is revealed in its name: frog legs provençal from the province of Provence; salad niçoise, with olives, anchovies, tomatoes, and tuna, from the city of Nice; beef *bourguignon*, beef stew with onions and mushrooms simmered in red wine, from the province of Burgundy; quiche lorraine, a custard tart with bacon and cheese, from the province of Lorraine; calf's head *à la lyonnaise*, with chopped onions and parsley, as served in the city of Lyon; and veal *à la normande*, made with cream and Calvados apple brandy, from Normandy.

Provençal dishes often contain onions, garlic, tomatoes, and olives. An Alsatian dish, on the other hand, probably has sauerkraut somewhere in the recipe and is washed down with beer instead of wine. Périgourdine ("pay-ree-gohr-DEEN") means there are luscious and expensive black truffles from Périgord in the sauce.

The cheeses of France often bear the name of the town where they are made, such as the world-famous blue-veined Roquefort made from ewe's milk and ripened in caves. France is known for Camembert, Brie, Port Salut ("POR sah-LEWH"), and more than 300 other kinds of cheeses, many of which are exported. The various cheeses made from goats' milk are called *chèvres* ("SHEVR").

The *cassoulet* is a French culinary classic. Experts say that a true *cassoulet* must consist of 30 percent pork sausage, mutton, or goose, with the remaining ingredients being white haricot beans, pork rinds, stock, and flavorings. The ingredients are pre-cooked separately in stages, then baked in layers in an earthenware pot known as a *cassole*.

CAFÉS, BRASSERIES, BISTROS

The habit of sitting at a café table for gossip and socializing is deeply ingrained in French society.

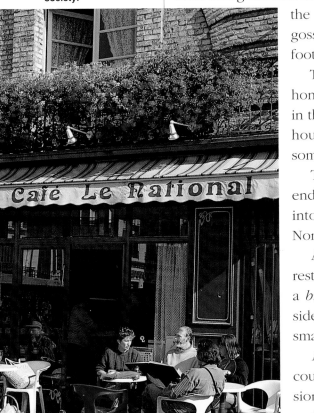

There are many wonderful places to eat at in France. Cafés offer drinks and snacks and, in the larger cities, light meals. They may have outdoor seats along the sidewalk. Cafés are open long hours, sometimes around the clock, making them a popular spot to linger for gossip and perhaps a game of chess, dominoes, or table football.

The bistro ranges from the simple bar to the time-honored old restaurant with faithful patrons. Reflected in the decorated mirrors, waiters in blue aprons serve house specialties, omelets, steak with fries, and sometimes much fancier foods.

The neighborhood café or bistro may be an endangered species, since so many are converting into fast-food places, fashionable restaurants, or North African kebab stalls.

A *brasserie* ("BRASS-uh-REE") is a large, busy restaurant with waiters in white aprons. Traditionally, a *brasserie* brewed beer; the cuisine is on the heavier side, with many Alsatian and seafood dishes. Tables are small and arranged in a cosy fashion.

An *auberge* ("oh-BEHRZH") is an inn, usually in the country, serving drinks and complete meals. Occasionally they accommodate customers for the night.

Customary hours for most French restaurants are noon to 2:30 P.M. and 7 to 10 P.M., with later closings in Paris. Menus with prices are often freshly handwritten each day and are posted outside the restaurants.

EATING THROUGH THE DAY

In France, families start the day with a small breakfast that usually consists of bread with butter and jam. They drink black coffee, coffee with hot milk, or the children's favorite—hot chocolate. Flaky, crescent-shaped rolls called croissants appear as a special treat.

The main meal of the day is often eaten at noon, during the two-hour lunch break. It consists of several courses, beginning with an appetizer or soup. Steaks with French-fried potatoes or roast chicken served with vegetables are popular main courses. The salad, usually made of greens tossed with oil-and-vinegar dressing, follows as a separate course. A selection of cheeses may come next, and then fresh fruit or a pastry dessert to complete the meal.

People who do not go home for the midday meal may eat a lighter lunch of a quiche or sandwich in a restaurant. The evening meal, whether called dinner or supper, may be simpler than the large midday meal. A typical menu would be soup, a casserole, and bread and cheese.

There are hundreds of different varieties of cheeses to choose from in France. The most widely eaten is Camembert, a soft cow's-milk cheese with a whitish rind.

Bread is eaten with meals. There are many varieties of bread, but the crusty *baguette* is the most common.

Wine is usually served at lunch and dinner. Mineral water, plain or carbonated, may also be served. At festive meals, a different wine may be served with each course. Champagne is usually brought out for special occasions. After-dinner brandies or sweet drinks called liqueurs may be offered, along with strong black coffee served in small cups. The French add sugar but not cream to this coffee. At a very formal meal, a fish course comes between the appetizer and the meat.

Long, crisp loaves of French bread, called baguettes, accompany meals. Because this bread has no preservatives, the French buy it fresh each day. Brioche is a popular sweet, soft dinner bun.

Sunday dinners and grand occasions call for impressive desserts, such as the famed French pastries in a dazzling variety of shapes and flavors. Popular choices are fruit tarts, éclairs, and thin pancakes with sweet fillings. There are regional specialties and also desserts reserved for certain holidays and celebrations.

Like most Europeans, the French cut and eat food with the fork in their left hand and the knife in their right. They break off chunks of bread instead of slicing the baguette. Because the French love to talk, mealtimes are often very animated with interesting conversations.

France produces a quarter of the world's wines, and the French are the biggest drinkers of wine per capita in the world.

WINES AND OTHER SPIRITS

France is famous for its excellent wines and bubbly champagnes. There are several important wine-producing regions, and each one makes a unique kind of wine. The shape of its bottle tells where a wine was made: Burgundy, Bordeaux, Alsace, Provence, or the Rhône Valley.

The year on a wine bottle is important, because changing weather conditions affect the flavor of the grapes. The prices also vary from year to year, with the greatest wines costing hundreds of dollars per bottle. Ordinary table wines are quite inexpensive.

Some wines improve with age and must rest in their bottles for years. Others can be drunk young. Many vineyards maintain huge wine cellars and offer tastings to the public in their tasting cellars.

Because French wines are so important to French prestige and the economy, the government inspects them to maintain their quality. Labels with the letters "AOC" indicate that a wine has been officially approved.

France also produces beer and cider. Other drinks called *apéritifs* ("ah-peh-ri-TEEF") are drunk before meals. *Pernod* ("pehr-NOH") and *pastis* ("pahs-TEES") have an anise flavor and are quite popular. After-dinner brandies such as Armagnac and Cognac are commonly drunk.

FRENCH ONION SOUP (*SOUPE A L'OIGNON AU FROMAGE*)

This recipe serves eight people.

4 ounces (113 g) butter or
    margarine
4–5 thinly sliced onions
2 tablespoons flour
½ cup white wine
4 cans (10 ounces or 296 ml
    each) condensed beef
    broth
4 cans (10 ounces or 296 ml
    each) condensed chicken
    broth
10 cups water
½ teaspoon black pepper
½ teaspoon thyme
4 baguette slices
3 ounces (80 g) grated or
    sliced Swiss cheese

Melt butter or margarine in a deep saucepan on medium heat with the sliced onions. Mix the onions with the butter and tenderize the onions for about five minutes. Sprinkle the flour over the onions and mix. Add the white wine and mix. Add all the broth and water as well as the pepper and thyme. Cover and simmer on low heat for about 30 to 40 minutes. Toast the baguette slices. Sprinkle the Swiss cheese on top of the toasted bread slices, and line the bottom of eight soup bowls with the slices of bread. Pour the hot soup over the bread slices, and they will rise to the top.

TARTE TATIN

This French apple tart gets its name from the legend of the Tatin sisters, who loved to bake for their guests. One day the tart they were making toppled over in the oven. The two sisters served it nonetheless, giving their name to one of the most popular pastries around the country.

1 cup flour
12 tablespoons chilled butter,
   cut in bits
Sprinkle of salt
1 tablespoon plus 1 $^1/_2$ cups sugar

$^1/_4$ cup chilled water
4–6 apples, quartered
Juice of 1 lemon
Whipped cream, vanilla ice cream, or raspberry
   sauce and mint leaves (optional)

Put flour, 6 tablespoons butter, salt, and 1 tablespoon sugar in a food processor and blend for not more than 10 seconds. Add water and process again for not more than 10 seconds. The resulting dough should be lumpy and not too dry. Shape the dough in a circle, wrap in plastic, and chill for two hours in the refrigerator. Leave apples in lemon juice and half a cup of sugar in a bowl for about half an hour, then drain apples. In a small pan, melt remaining butter and sugar over low heat. Stir and cook until the mixture bubbles and changes color. Add a little water if necessary. Remove the pan from the heat and arrange the apples over the caramel. Return the pan to the heat and cook for about 25 minutes. Press the apples to spread the juice in the pan. When the juices are thick and syrupy, remove from the heat. Unwrap the dough and drape over the apples. Poke

six holes in the dough to allow steam to escape. Sprinkle with a bit of sugar. Bake for no more than 30 minutes until pastry turns golden-brown and crispy. Place a plate upside down over the pan and carefully turn both over so that the dough is now at the bottom and the apples on top. Serve with whipped cream on top or ice cream or raspberry sauce and mint leaves on the side.

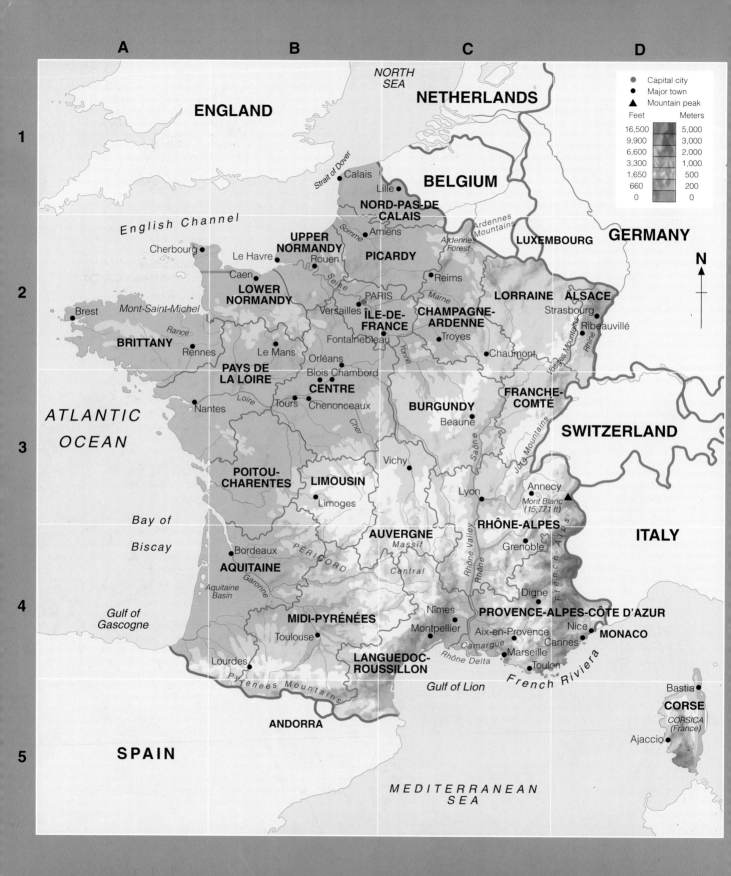

A B C D

NORTH
SEA

ENGLAND

NETHERLANDS

BELGIUM

GERMANY

1

Strait of Dover

Calais
Lille

NORD-PAS-DE
CALAIS

Somme

Amiens

Ardennes
Mountains

Ardennes
Forest

LUXEMBOURG

Capital city
Major town
Mountain peak

Feet   Meters
16,500   5,000
9,900   3,000
6,600   2,000
3,300   1,000
1,650   500
660   200
0   0

N

English Channel

Cherbourg

Le Havre

Caen

UPPER
NORMANDY

Rouen

PICARDY

Reims

LORRAINE   ALSACE

Strasbourg

Ribeauvillé

Rhine

2

Brest

Mont-Saint-Michel

LOWER
NORMANDY

Seine

PARIS

Versailles

ÎLE-DE-
FRANCE

Marne

CHAMPAGNE-
ARDENNE

Troyes

Chaumont

Vosges Mountains

Rance

BRITTANY

Rennes

Le Mans

Fontainebleau

PAYS DE
LA LOIRE

Orléans

Blois Chambord

CENTRE

Yonne

BURGUNDY

FRANCHE-
COMTÉ

ATLANTIC

OCEAN

Loire

Tours

Chenonceaux

Cher

Beaune

Saône

Jura Mountains

SWITZERLAND

3

Nantes

Vichy

POITOU-
CHARENTES

LIMOUSIN

Limoges

Lyon

Annecy

Mont Blanc
(15,771 ft)

ITALY

Bay of

Biscay

AUVERGNE

Massif

RHÔNE-ALPES

Grenoble

Rhône Valley

French Alps

Bordeaux

PÉRIGORD

Central

Digne

Rhône

4

Gulf of
Gascogne

AQUITAINE

Aquitaine
Basin

Garonne

MIDI-PYRÉNÉES

Toulouse

Nîmes

Montpellier

PROVENCE-ALPES-CÔTE D'AZUR

Aix-en-Provence

Nice

Cannes

MONACO

Camargue

Marseille

Lourdes

LANGUEDOC-
ROUSSILLON

Rhône Delta

Toulon

French Riviera

Bastia

Pyrenees Mountains

Gulf of Lion

CORSE

CORSICA
(France)

ANDORRA

MEDITERRANEAN
SEA

Ajaccio

5

SPAIN

MAP OF FRANCE

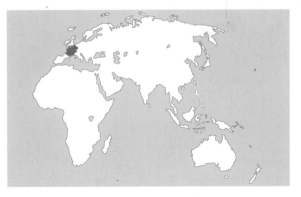

ECONOMIC FRANCE

Services

 Airport

 Eurotunnel

 Port

 Tourism

Manufacturing

 Aircraft

 Chemicals

 Textiles

 Vehicles

Natural Resources

 Aluminum

Iron and Steel

Nuclear Reactor

Farming

 Dairy Products

Sugar Beet

Wheat

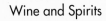 Wine and Spirits

ABOUT THE ECONOMY

OVERVIEW
The French government is releasing its control on the economy to market mechanisms, with the exception of the power, public transportation, and defense industries. The telecommunications sector, in particular, is opening up to competition.

GDP
US$1.2 trillion (2001)

GDP SECTORS
Agriculture 3 percent, industry 26 percent, services 71 percent

POPULATION
61.1 million, including 1.7 million in overseas departments and territories (2002)

LABOR FORCE
26 million (2001)

CURRENCY
The euro (EUR) replaced the French franc (FRF) in 2002 at a fixed rate of 6.55957 French francs per euro.
1 euro (EUR) = 100 cents
USD1 = EUR1.03 (August 2002)
Notes: 5, 10, 20, 50, 100, 200, 500 euros
Coins: 1, 2, 5, 10, 20, 50 cents; 1,2 euros

UNEMPLOYMENT
8.8 percent (2002)

MAJOR TRADE PARTNERS
Germany, Spain, the United Kingdom, Italy, the United States, Belgium, Netherlands, Luxembourg

MAIN EXPORTS
Aircraft, high technology, industrial and military equipment, wine, pharmaceutical products, chemicals, plastics, luxury products

MAIN IMPORTS
Oil, electricity, minerals, tropical food (coffee and fruit), machinery and equipment, aircraft, chemicals, plastics, vehicles

MAIN ENERGY SOURCE
Most (75 percent) of France's electricity comes from its 57 nuclear power plants. France is the world's largest nuclear power generator on a per capita basis.

COMMUNICATIONS MEDIA
Internet: 20 percent of households; 22 service providers (2002)

MAJOR AIRPORTS
14

PORTS AND HARBORS
Boulogne, Calais, Cherbourg, Dunkerque, La Rochelle, Le Havre, Lyon, Marseille, Mullhouse, Nantes, Paris, Saint Nazaire, Strasbourg, Toulon

CULTURAL FRANCE

Parc Astérix
Based on a famous comic character, Asterix the Gaul, this entertainment theme park 19 miles (30 km) north of Paris attracts families from all over the country when spring comes.

Mont-Saint-Michel
This is a circular rocky islet off the coast of Lower Normandy, north of Rennes. An oratory was built here in the eighth century by St. Aubert, bishop of Avranches, after having a vision of the archangel Michael. The island was fortified in 1256 and resisted seiges during the Hundred Years' War and the French Wars of Religion. Napoleon used it as a state prison. In 1862 Mont-Saint-Michel was classified as a Historical Monument by the French and in 1979 UNESCO declared it a World Heritage site.

Disneyland Resort Paris
This Disneyland theme park attracts about 12 million visitors every year. It is located east of Paris, just 35 minutes away by Métro.

Cathedral of Amiens
One of the biggest Romanesque and Gothic cathedrals in France, famous for its elaborate and creative sculptures, such as its splendid rose windows and soaring nave. Building began in 1220 and was completed about 50 years later.

Eiffel Tower
Built for France's Centennial Exposition of 1889, it was never brought down and became Paris's favorite tourist landmark.

Notre Dame Cathedral
This impressive Gothic cathedral was built in Paris during the Middle Ages and modified through the centuries. It is best known as the home of the Hunchback of Notre Dame from a novel by Victor Hugo.

Louvre Museum
Formerly a palace for French kings, it is now a famous international museum in Paris, home to the mysterious Mona Lisa.

Palace of Versailles
The favorite castle of Louis XIV, the Sun King, built in the 17th century and famous for its gardens and water plays. The Treaty of Versailles was signed here, in the Hall of Mirrors, in 1919 by the Allied and Associated Powers and by Germany. This palace still serves as a residence for visiting heads of state.

24 Hours of Le Mans
Every year the biggest and longest auto race takes place here in the city of Le Mans. Lasting seven days, the 70th race was held in 2002.

Lascaux/Lascaux II caves
Discovered by some youths in 1940, its cave paintings of horses, stags, aurochs, ibex, and bison are famous. It is now closed to the public and reproductions of these paintings have been built next to the original cave.

Arc de Triomphe
A famous Parisian monument celebrating Napoleon's military victories during the French Revolution.

Chateau of Chambord
This fairytale chateau is the largest of a string of ravishing Renaissance chateaux along the Loire River: Chenonceaux, Amboise, Blois, Cheverny, and Ussé. It was rebuilt by Francis I and Henry II, and Molière wrote here.

Lourdes
Some 6 million pilgrims visit Lourdes every year, where the Virgin Mary allegedly appeared in 1858. This site has a reputation for miracle healings.

Film Festival of Cannes
Started in 1946 and held every year in spring, this film festival in Cannes, near Nice, draws the *crème de la crème* of international actors and movie-makers.

ABOUT THE CULTURE

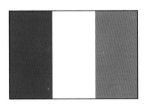

OFFICIAL NAME
French Republic

CAPITAL
Paris

NATIONAL FLAG
Adopted in the earlier days of the 1789 French Revolution, the tricolor French flag symbolizes royalty (white) and the capital, Paris (red and blue).

NATIONAL ANTHEM
La Marseillaise ("Lah Mar-say-yez"), or *The Song of Marseilles*. A rousing tune composed by Claude Joseph Rouget de Lisle in 1792, written to motivate revolution and inspire patriotism.

NATIONAL MOTTO
Liberté, Égalité, Fraternité (Liberty, Equality, and Brotherhood)

ETHNIC GROUPS
Celtic and Latin majorities, with Teutonic, Slavic, North African, Indochinese, and Basque minorities

RELIGIOUS GROUPS
Roman Catholic, Muslim, Protestant, Jewish

LANGUAGES
French. Main regional dialects: Alsatian, Basque, Breton, Catalan, Corsican, Flemish, Provençal

LIFE EXPECTANCY
75 years for men, 83 years for women (2001 est.)

SYSTEM OF GOVERNMENT
Known as the Fifth Republic, a parliamentary democracy with a president elected by voters for a five-year term. The executive branch is the National Assembly, with 577 members elected for five-year terms by direct regional universal suffrage.

IMPORTANT ANNIVERSARIES
Labor Day (May 1), Victory Day (May 8), Bastille Day (July 14), Armistice Day (November 12)

LEADERS IN POLITICS
Jacques Chirac—president (elected in 1995, 2002)
Jean-Pierre Raffarin—prime minister (elected in 2002)

OTHER FAMOUS PEOPLE
Victor Hugo (1802–85)—poet, novelist, and dramatist who wrote *Les Misérables* and *Notre-Dame de Paris*
Louis Pasteur (1822–95)—chemist and micro-biologist; inventor of pasteurization
Pierre-Auguste Renoir (1841–1919)—Impressionist painter
Jacques-Yves Cousteau (1910–97)—ocean explorer; inventor of aqualung diving apparatus and underwater television

TIME LINE

IN FRANCE	IN THE WORLD
17,000 B.C. Painting of the Lascaux caves	
	753 B.C. Rome is founded.
	116–17 B.C. The Roman Empire reaches its greatest extent, under Emperor Trajan (98–17).
58–51 B.C. Julius Caesar invades Gaul.	
A.D. 486 First Frankish kingdom established by Clovis	**A.D. 600** Height of Mayan civilization
A.D. 771–814 Reign of Charlemagne, the greatest Carolingian ruler	
A.D. 800 Opening of the first public schools	
A.D. 987–996 Hugh Capet is named the first in a line of 13 Capetian kings.	**1000** The Chinese perfect gunpowder and begin to use it in warfare.
1163–1350 Construction of Notre-Dame Cathedral in Paris	
1337 Start of the Hundred Years' War with the English	
1430–31 Trial of Joan of Arc; she is burned at the stake in Rouen at the age of 19.	**1453** Turks take Constantinople, marking the end of the Byzantine Empire and the rise of the Ottoman Empire.
	1492 Christopher Columbus discovers America.
	1620 Pilgrim Fathers sail the *Mayflower* to America.
1643–1715 Reign of Louis the XIV, the Sun King	
1777 Marquis de Lafayette fights alongside George Washington for U.S. independence.	**1776** U.S. Declaration of Independence.

IN FRANCE	IN THE WORLD

1789
French Revolution begins.

1793
King Louis XVI and Queen Marie-Antoinette are guillotined. The First Republic is formed.

1799
Napoleon becomes emperor.

1861
U.S. Civil War begins.

1869
The Suez Canal is opened.

1870–71
War with Prussia. France loses Alsace and Lorraine.

1889
The Eiffel Tower is erected.

1914
World War I begins.

1918
The first Armistice Day. France recovers lost regions.

1933
Hitler rises to power in Germany.

1939
World War II begins.

1940
France surrenders to Germany.

1944
D-Day. The Allied forces land on the shores of Normandy to liberate France.

1945
The United States drops atomic bombs on Hiroshima and Nagasaki.

1949
North Atlantic Treaty Organization (NATO) is formed.

1966–69
Chinese Cultural Revolution

1969
Charles de Gaulle retires.

1981
François Mitterrand is elected president.

1991
Break-up of the Soviet Union

2002
Replacement of the French franc with the euro. Jacques Chirac is reelected president instead of right extremist Jean-Marie Le Pen.

2001
World population surpasses 6 billion. World Trade Center terrorist attacks in the United States.

GLOSSARY

apéritif ("ah-peh-ri-TEEF")
An alcoholic drink taken as an appetizer.

auberge ("oh-BEHRZH")
An inn, usually in the country, serving drinks, complete meals, and sometimes lodging.

bistro ("BEES-troh")
An intimate eatery with waiters, typically in dark blue aprons, serving house specialties.

bonjour ("bawn-ZHOOR")
"Hello." An everyday greeting.

boules ("BOO-luh")
A game of bowling without pins, popular in southern France.

brasserie ("BRASS-uh-ree")
A large restaurant with waiters in white aprons.

brioche ("bree-OCH-uh")
A sweet, soft bun.

charcuterie ("shar-kye-tuh-REE")
Cooked meat, usually pork (hams, sausages, pâtés), or a shop selling these.

château ("SHAH-toe")
A castle or grand country home.

crêpe ("KREH-puh")
A thin pancake, served with either sweet or savoury toppings and/or stuffing.

cuisine minceur ("kwee-ZEEN man-SOOR")
Low-calorie dishes for the weight-conscious.

gendarmes ("zhawn-DAHR-muh")
State police serving in the armed forces.

grandes écoles ("GRAHN-dzay-KOHL")
Elite colleges.

haute cuisine ("OAT kwee-ZEEN")
Elaborate dishes.

joie de vivre ("JWAH duh VE-vruh")
Love of life, joy in living.

madame ("mah-DAHM")
Mrs., Madam.

mademoiselle ("mahd-mwah-ZEHL")
Miss, young lady.

monsieur ("muh-SYUH")
Mr., Sir

nouvelle cuisine ("noo-VELL kwee-ZEEN")
Dishes prepared with light sauces, using less butter, cream, and flour.

savoir faire ("SAH-vwahr FAIR")
Ability to respond appropriately in any situation.

tabac ("tah-BAHK")
Tobacco, or a shop selling newspapers, stamps, and cigarettes.

FURTHER INFORMATION

BOOKS

Braudel, Fernand. *The Identity of France, Volume One: History and Environment.* New York: Harper Collins Trade, 1990.

Delaforce, Patrick. *The Nature Parks of France.* Northampton, MA: Interlink Publishing Group,1996.

Ingham, Richard. *Nations of the World: France.* New York: Raintree Steck-Vaughan, 2000.

WEBSITES

Central Intelligence Agency World Factbook (select "France" from the country list). www.cia.gov/cia/publications/factbook

Energy Information Administration (EIA) website's France Country Analysis Brief. www.eia.doe.gov/emeu/cabs/france.html

French Agency for Environment and Energy Management. www.ademe.fr/anglais/vadefault.htm

French Institute for the Environment. www.ifen.fr/english/index.htm

French Ministry of Defense. www.defense.gouv.fr/english/index_ang.html

French Ministry of the Environment. www.environnement.gouv.fr/english/default.htm

French Ministry of Foreign Affairs. www.diplomatie.gouv.fr/index.gb.html

Ministry for Social Affairs, Work, and Solidarity. www.travail.gouv.fr

Ministry of the Economy, Finance, and Industry. www.finances.gouv.fr/minefi/minefi_ang/index.htm

National Assembly. www.assemblee-nat.fr/english/index.asp

National Institute of Statistics and Economic Studies. www.insee.fr

Parcs Nationaux de France. www.parcsnationaux-fr.com

Planet Ark. www.planetark.org/dailynewsstory.cfm/newsid/15292/story.htm

Presidency of the French Republic. www.elysee.fr/ang/index.shtm

Prime Minister and Government of France. www.premier-ministre.gouv.fr/en

Senate. www.senat.fr/english/somm.html

MUSIC

Pavane: Ravel, Satie, Fauré. Orpheus Chamber Orchestra. Polygram Records, 1997.

Voice of the Sparrow: The Very Best of Edith Piaf. Capitol, 1991.

VIDEOS

Biography: Napoleon Bonaparte—The Glory of France. Home Video, 2000.

France: The Visit. Home Vision Entertainment, 2000.

Manon of the Springs. MGM, 1987.

BIBLIOGRAPHY

Ardagh, John and Colin Jones. *Cultural Atlas of France*. New York: Facts on File, 1991.

Bailey, Rosemary (project editor). *Dorling Kindersley Travel Guides: France*. New York: Dorling Kindersley, 2002.

Bernstein, Richard. *Fragile Glory: A Portrait of France and the French*. New York: Alfred A. Knopf, 1990.

Mayle, Peter. *A Year in Provence*. New York: Alfred A. Knopf, 1990.

Mitchell, Crohan. *The Napoleonic Wars*. New York: David and Charles, 1989.

Mulvahill, Margaret. *The French Revolution*. New York: Franklin Watts, 1989.

Popkin, Jeremy D. *History of Modern France*. 2nd edition. London: University of Kentucky, Pearson Education, 2001.

Rambali, Paul. *French Blues: A Not-so Sentimental Journey Through Lives and Memories in Modern France*. London: Heinemann, 1989.

Weber, Eugen Joseph. *My France: Politics, Culture, Myth*. Cambridge: Belknap Press of Harvard University Press, 1991.

INDEX